We Are One

Stories of Soccer, Courage, & Hope from Nigeria, West Africa

Compiled by Adam Miles
Designed by Molly Green
Edited by Adam Miles, Katherin Kennedy &
Melissa Marsted
Photographs by Travis J Photography

Published by:

Bridges To Your Best LLC
Park City, UT
adam@bridgestoyourbest.com

Text and Illustrations Copyright ©2015 Bridges to Your Best LLC

A large portion of the proceeds of *We Are One* will benefit our social impact venture: Save-A-Thon For Africa

www.bridgestoamerica.org
www.saveathonforafrica.org

ISBN 978-0692426371

We Are One

Stories of Soccer, Courage, & Hope
from Nigeria, West Africa

SAVE-A-TH⚽N
-BRIDGES TO AMERICA-

Table of Contents

INTRODUCTION 5

MAP OF NIGERIA 9

WHAT IS BRIDGES TO AMERICA? 10

WHAT IS SAVE-A-THON FOR AFRICA? 11

PREPARATION 12

COMMITMENT 20

FUNDRAISING 25

TAKING OFF 30

ON THE GROUND 34

THE JOURNEY TO OSUN 51

SOCCER CLINIC 55

DAY OF SERVICE 66

GAME ON 87

RELAXING AT ZENABABS 93

GOING AWAY PARTY 94

LAST DAY 97

WRAPPING UP 102

OBSERVATIONS 103

DICKSON 112

ADAM on DICKSON..114

CONCLUSION 116

TIMELINE 123

INTRODUCTION

A promise.

A simple promise.

Two years ago I was visiting Africa for the very first time. On this trip I met a nice young boy living in a poor village well outside of Accra, the capital of Ghana. He asked me if I had a soccer ball for him. I didn't.

But I was touched by this simple request and ashamed I had nothing to give him. In that moment I promised him that I would bring him and his friends soccer balls from America. I got excited thinking about my twelve-year-old daughter, Kylie, 8,000 miles away back home in Utah and how, with this promise, I could bring together her love of soccer and her desire to help people. Save-A-Thon For Africa was born.

Like most people, I am not independently wealthy, and I lead a very busy life: two great excuses to not keep that promise. This little boy would never be able to find me and hold me accountable for my promise if I simply went home and forgot about him. But that's not who I am and I knew I just had to keep that promise.

When I returned home and told my family, and specifically Kylie, of this event and this promise I could literally see this boy's face and could hear myself in my mind making this crazy promise. Looking back on it, I really had no right or position in life to make it. But one thing about me is that I hate when someone makes a promise and then breaks it. To me it's the same thing as lying. Doing what you say you will do is called integrity and it has always been an important part of whom I have tried to be all my life. So many people today say things and then, for whatever reason, don't follow through. I believe doing what you say is THE key to success in life. (That's a topic for another another time.)

Well, this simple promise made in the midst of the unique emotions one feels seeing innocent, good kids living in terrible poverty with very little to hope for led me to take actions that I had never taken before. With Kylie's help, and the help of many family members and friends, we told the world about our plans; we raised money; we bought expensive plane tickets; and we traveled half way around the world the day after my eldest daughter, Mikaelyn, was married and just six days before Christmas. It was an amazing journey that was truly filled with a lot of hard work, determination, and a few sleepless nights.

With the help of many supporters and the hard work of Kylie saving goals to raise money, my simple promise was kept.

Fast forward to December 2013 and I am sitting in a meeting room in Logan, Utah introducing, pitching really, about 20 young female soccer players and their parents the idea of raising money, lots of it, to travel to Nigeria to play soccer against other female players there and perform humanitarian service. The fact that I wasn't laughed out of the room that night says a lot about the girls, some of whom would eventually join the trip, and their parents, who would support them.

Three months later in March, 2014, I was humbled and sort of amazed to lead a group of 20 volunteers with a core of 13 brave, outstanding American young women on a life-changing trip to Nigeria. I still really can't believe the good these girls accomplished in our week-long journey in Africa, but what they did on this trip not only changed their lives but also made the world a better place.

My simple promise made two years earlier turned into something remarkable. In these pages these wonderful young women give the details of our trip as they experienced it, from start to finish, as they believed in my promise and desired to make their own promises and commitments. You will read the mission of Save-A-Thon For Africa in action: the effort of dozens of American teenage girls to inspire thousands of youth in Africa and the US to be better than they are today, the opportunity to build relationships through the world's sport of soccer and the importance of making and keeping promises despite how hard that may be.

These girls inspire me and truly are my heroes. I can't wait for you to get to know them through their stories. I hope you will share what you read with others.

The profits from the sales of this book will go directly to Bridges To America so that we can continue to keep promises and make the world a better place one child at a time.

Adam Miles

Founder and Executive Director
Bridges To America, Inc.

MAP OF NIGERIA

What is Bridges To America?

Bridges To America, Inc. is a registered 501(c)(3) entity started by Adam Miles in 2004 with the primary mission of aiding African families. Originally this aid was provided in the form of reunification services for family members who have been separated by poverty, war, famine, etc. and are stuck in Africa. Frequent flyer miles and/or money are raised and donated to provide airfare to legally join a family member living in the United States. To date more than six families have been reunited through these efforts and all of these families are working hard to make the most of their opportunity to live in the United States.

The joy of reuniting families is very fulfilling but the opportunities to help weren't coming often enough. So, a decision was made to take a more proactive approach in aiding African families and **Save-A-Thon For Africa** was born.

More information about Bridges To America is available at:

www.bridgestoamerica.org.

Donations to Bridges To America are tax deductible in the US.

What is Save-A-Thon For Africa?

Save-A-Thon For Africa is a unique social impact venture operating in both the USA and Nigeria. Our mission is to:

<u>Educate and Empower Young Women Through Soccer</u>

We accomplish our mission in several ways:

1. Under the guidance and financial support of Bridges To America and its supporters, <u>free youth soccer clinics</u> are conducted throughout communities in Nigeria by young <u>American women volunteers</u>, mostly soccer players, who raise their own funds to travel there to engage these youth, especially girls, to develop relationships and inspire them.

2. Bridges To America organizes regular youth soccer tournaments in Nigeria for competitive players called the <u>Bridges Cup</u>. Teams compete for prizes and pride with the winning boys team and the winning girls team receiving a week-long trip to play soccer in America.

3. The <u>Bridges Cup USA</u> is a youth soccer event held to welcome the winning boys and girls teams of the Bridges Cup from Nigeria to the USA. Friendly matches are organized and played against the best state teams. Also, the Nigerian youth are introduced to American schools, businesses, governments, and cultural sites.

4. Longer-term we will build the <u>Save-A-Thon School for Girls</u> and provide life-changing opportunities for learning, empowerment, growth and leadership.

More information and opportunities to help with the Save-A-Thon For Africa project can be found at <u>www.saveathonforafrica.org</u>

SAVE-A-TH⚽N
-BRIDGES TO AMERICA-

Preparation

Hopes, Fears, and Hard Work

The team only spent one week on the actual trip but they spent several months in preparation. This was the period during which they truly showed their commitment to the project and did the hard work that enabled them to take this amazing journey. This period of work and preparation is a lot like training for a soccer game. You work for weeks and even months for a ninety minute game. No matter how much you put into the preparation phase, which by the way is rarely fun, determines the quality of the actual event: the game, or in this case, the actual trip to Africa.

Here is how these amazing young ladies prepared for their journey and what they thought during the process.

Why are you going to Nigeria and what do you hope to accomplish?

Kaycee Larsen, 13

I want to go to Africa to make a difference. If there's anything I've learned from preparing for this trip, it's that one person can make a huge difference. That's what I want to do. I also want to meet new people and gain a perspective on how life is in Nigeria.

Personally I want to have new things shown to me. I want to go and see how little they have, and how they are still happy. I want to learn to live like that.

People have told me the experience will include life-changing things; things there you don't even dream about here. There will be poverty, danger, sickness and pain. I think it will be hard to see.

Tabitha Smith, 13

Yes, I know what you are probably thinking, "Holy cow! Why would I travel almost 8,000 miles to go somewhere with so much less than what we have here in America?"

But, for me, it was a no brainer. Ever since my mother traveled to India to do humanitarian work, I have been inspired to do something along those lines. When our soccer team's goalie's father (and founder of Bridges To America) made the proposal there was no way I could refuse. I knew going in that I could not help everybody there, but I did try to help the people I met. Sometimes my acts were small, like a wave or a smile or as large as giving the soccer cleats (or boots as they called them) off my feet. The smallest things to them were worth so much.

One of the scariest things for me was thinking about all the starving kids I might see and knowing that I couldn't take them all (or as a matter of fact any of them) home with me.

Maizy Stull, 13

It has been my life's dream to travel the world! When I was given the opportunity to travel to Africa with a purpose, I was thrilled and knew right away that I just HAD to go on this trip.

I hope to inspire the young women in Africa to use the love of soccer to lift their lives, like my teammates and I do.

I think that I will see poverty everywhere. I know that African countries are somewhat third world, and it wouldn't surprise me if Nigeria was also one. I'm also nervous about unfamiliar bugs and diseases.

Kylie Miles, 13

The main thing that I am hoping to accomplish is to put smiles on the faces of these beautiful Nigerian kids. I want to give them opportunities and inspire them to go out and work for whatever it is that they want in life or whatever they have a passion for. I also want my soccer team to experience the Nigerian culture, and I hope all of our lives will be changed.

This is my third trip to Africa and I love going there because of how different it is from the US. It's always so cool to experience their culture and see the way they do things differently. It's also very humbling to experience the way they live with almost nothing compared to everything we have in America.

Britnee West, 17

I can't believe in five days I will be on a plane headed to a completely different continent to change lives. It still doesn't seem real to me. I have wanted to have this experience for as long as I can remember. I'm so excited my dream is coming true!

Preparing for this trip has me thinking about how best I can help these people and children who have absolutely nothing. What can I bring them that will help change their lives? I have decided to bring them lots of clothes, toys, soccer balls, and candy. I am excited to share the game of soccer with these kids because I believe the game can truly help them better their lives. It has been a huge part of my life, and I don't know what I would have done without it.

I want to have this experience because I know it will change my life. Seeing a completely different culture will be an amazing experience for me, and I could not be more excited! I hope to be greatly humbled by the things I see in Nigeria. I know it will make me very grateful for what I have, and I hope to see that I was able to help other people.

Noheli Mora, 13

I wanted to take this trip because I thought it would be a great experience for me that would also help me in the future. I thought going would make me grateful for the things I have in the United States. It will also be great to learn and experience their culture while we are there.

I hope that by going I will learn to be more grateful in what I have in life and also to be more polite and to communicate with others better. I also hope to become more responsible because I am going alone and have to be responsible for my things and myself. I also look forward to getting to know my teammates better.

Bizzy Oldham, 13

So far I am super excited to go to Nigeria! I can't wait to get there and see all the people and places there. I've done some fundraising and knocked on doors for donations. I think this is a very special opportunity. I'm also blessed that my sister and many of my teammates will be joining me on this trip. I'm so thankful for my amazing parents for letting me go on this trip. It seems like I have been waiting for this trip for a long time. I know that this trip will change my life forever.

Hanna Peterson, 13

I can't wait. I haven't even started packing yet. And we leave in a little more than two days. My dad and I went out fundraising yesterday and the day before. We've also sold soccer shin guard sleeves. I think we've raised $436. We're going to use this money to fill the suitcases with toys and school supplies for the kids there. I literally cannot wait. It's going to be such an eye-opening experience. I have to go to bed now. Good night. I'm so excited. I'm going to Africa!!!

Hailey Oldham, 17

Before I head off on my trip to Nigeria, I hope I can affect their lives in a positive way and compare and contrast my life with theirs. I think Africa will be very run-down and not clean. It will be hot and humid. I think the people of Nigeria will be kind and grateful for what we bring and what we are doing for them and accept us when we get there.

I am afraid that crowds of people will bombard us , and I'll feel bad if I won't be able to give them something. I am so pumped to go, and I'm sure my experience there will be amazing.

Marissa Miles, 18

I was fortunate enough to be able to go on the first Save-A-Thon trip to Ghana with my dad and sister and I absolutely fell in love with Africa and the project. Ever since then I was eager to get back there whenever I could and this motivated me to go on the trip to Nigeria with the soccer team.

Even though I don't play soccer, I am excited to go and interact with all the kids. I can't wait to serve the sweet spirits in Nigeria and learn more about myself while doing so. I know these will be life changing moments and memories I will hold onto forever.

Alex Hollingsworth, 18

<u>Adam:</u> As you will see, Alex contributed much to this book, but we somehow missed her thoughts for this section. So, let me give you two of my favorite quotes of hers that reflect what a champ she was on the trip:

"Bring it on, this trip will be life changing and I am so excited!"

"I want to help them and change their lives. They live these lives that they do because they don't know any better. We can help them see that what they have for a life isn't what it has to be. That there are better things out there, and that we care about them.

Megan Hollingsworth, 14

I am going to Africa to…spend a couple days in a completely new setting with new kinds of people who have a whole new perspective on the game. I am excited to see this all play out. I can't wait.

Lucy Christensen, 13

<u>Adam:</u> Lucy is quiet and a self-proclaimed "nonwriter" so you will only see her in photos throughout the book. But she and her dad, Ed, were an important part of our effort and we were fortunate to have them both with us in Nigeria. She displayed a great deal of love, respect, and heart to the kide there and I am proud of the impact she made.

Commitment

Adam

I love to read the girls' hopes as they made, and stuck with, the decision to take this risk and join me in my vision to impact the lives of thousands of youth in Nigeria through soccer. I was reminded through this huge effort that anything really valuable in life comes only through hard work and faith to make it through the tough times. I was faced with numerous people who said to me: "Nigeria?! Are you crazy?!" I became accustomed to those comments and the frequent looks from fellow passengers of "Are you sure you're on the right plane?" the many times I boarded the United Airlines flight in Houston bound for Lagos as just about the only white guy in the cabin.

These girls had never been to Nigeria. Some had never before left Utah. Plus, they are just kids. So, when they were inevitably faced with friends, families, donors, and strangers asking questions and some even casting doubt on whether this trip was such a good idea the girls had to make a choice: stick to their decision or get scared and back out.

I am so proud that each of these girls met negativity with courage and determination. The pages of this book are a testament to the rewards they received for doing so.

Tabitha

People constantly asked me why I would want to go to Nigeria. They told me how dangerous it was and asked if I would be safe when I went. They were all so scared that something bad was going to happen. Every day at school, one of my best friends would tell me to take lots of bug spray and that I was going to get sick from the bugs over there. I knew that my parents and Adam would never even suggest something like this trip if we weren't going to be safe. The closer I got to going the more people would tell me about all the wars and killing that was going on over there. My mom would remind me that if you took all the bad stuff that was happening here in America and left out the good then nobody would want to come here either.

Noheli

Honestly, it took a lot of courage because you never know what's going to happen there. I was pretty scared when we left. Once we got there, Adam told us not to let anybody touch our bags. I was afraid that someone was going to yank it out of my hands. I was also afraid of being kidnapped.

Maizy

Some people were supportive of my going to Nigeria and some weren't. I know most of them were a little worried, and a few were very nervous. I think what made them the most nervous was the news about the religious war going on up north. There were also a couple of people who just didn't think I should go at all. Their opinions were understandable, yet some were harsh. I didn't let them make me back down.

No one really tried to talk me out of going, yet some had very strong opinions on why I shouldn't go. I listened to the opinions and shrugged them off as worrying over nothing. I trusted that I would be safe.

It didn't really take much courage for me to go to Nigeria because I knew that most of the danger and trouble is found in the north, whereas we would be traveling south to the peaceful states. Also, the probability of something going wrong was very slim. My attitude was that there was nothing to worry about as long as we followed the rules and stayed safe.

Alex

When Adam first announced the possibility to be able to go to Nigeria in the spring of 2014, I was immediately all in, but there was always a part of me in the back of my head saying "There is no way that this is going to happen. Taking a group of very white, very blonde American girls into Africa?" As time got closer, it became real. It was really happening, and I was so excited. Everyone that we talked to asked, "Oh! Cool, what part?" and we would tell them Nigeria and their response each time was "Oh my gosh, please be careful; it is so dangerous over there." Each time I would just smile and say "Bring it on; it will be life-changing, and I am so excited!"

There was always a part of me that was nervous, but I was never scared. I knew that Nigeria was different than America in a lot of different ways, but to me it was never about myself. It was always about helping others, and helping others is never scary.

Kaycee

One day in February my dad casually told me that our soccer team, Logan Lynx, was going to Nigeria. We didn't know many details yet but we were excited and all in. But, as we learned more about some of the dangers in northern Nigeria, we slowly drifted towards not going; we weren't sure if the risk was worth the reward.

Suddenly, I had a choice to make. I had one week to tell Adam if I was in or not. My dad told me to pray and ask Heavenly Father what we should do. So I did. I prayed and asked Him every night but didn't receive an answer. The night before we were supposed to tell Adam, my dad and I had decided to not go. But, I prayed one last time, asking Him if it was the right decision to stay home.

I got an answer. He let me know that we could go, and He would protect us while we were there. I woke up the next day and went to talk to my dad. I went upstairs, and he was sitting in the kitchen. He asked me if I had prayed and I said, "Yes." He looked at me and said, "Be honest, what do you think?" He told me not to worry about anyone else and just worry about myself. I told him that I had been comforted. He said he had the exact same feeling. We told Adam that we were officially a part of Save-A-Thon for Africa!

FUNDRAISING

Adam

Had I known at the start just how ambitious or difficult this Save-A-Thon For Africa venture really would be I might have never started it. I guess ignorance really can be bliss! Well, I am grateful to find myself with just the right mix of naiveté, boldness, and crazy because in two short years this mix has been exactly what the effort has needed to go from an idea sparked one afternoon in the hot African sun to a successful project that has touched the lives of thousands of Africans and hundreds of Americans. You can likely imagine how expensive all of this must be. And you would be right! But what Kylie and I had started I simply could not stop. I knew that for this to work, for the Nigerians to want to be a part of this, we needed to get a team of American young women to Nigeria to play soccer with them.

At the same time, considering the risks and high costs of traveling to Nigeria I also knew I was asking a lot of the girls and their families. I tried to find a price level that was manageable for each girl to raise and yet wouldn't leave me broke paying for the difference. I decided that $1,500 would cover flights and hotels for the girls and each adult going on the trip would have to pay $2,000. Additionally, each person on the trip was responsible to cover the costs of their passports, visas, and vaccinations, which added another $500 or so.

Most of these girls did an amazing job of raising the necessary funds to pay their way to Nigeria. A few girls raised more than double the required $1,500. Tabitha's dad, Brandon Smith, wanted to accompany his daughter, and since, he is a nurse, we were delighted to have him. I didn't find out for a couple of months that he told Tabitha that if she wanted him to come she would have to raise his required $2,000 as well. Well, she did, and we were fortunate to have a nurse, and another great dad, on the trip.

Fundraising is the hardest element of any humanitarian effort and I can say without hesitation how much I admire these girls for their diligence in meeting their goal. More proof that young American women aren't afraid to work hard and that they don't shy away from doing difficult things.

By virtue of the book you are now holding you know that the dream of going to Nigeria was accomplished through the girls' perseverance. And in the aftermath of the kidnapping of over 250 Nigerian schoolgirls, the "Chibok Girls," in April 2014, these American girls have an even stronger desire to help. With profits from this book, they hope to provide funds to help young Nigerian girls have life-changing opportunities in their educational and soccer pursuits. Your purchase of this book helps us continue this work. Thank you.

Read on to see how these girls managed one of the most challenging aspects of their Save-A-Thon trip.

Kaycee

There was a lot of work to be done and at the beginning I was excited, but overwhelmed. I had to get money, passports, visas, and shots. We had to get food and clothes packed too. It was crazy. But it was a once-in-a-lifetime opportunity, and I was so happy to be a part of it.

For me the hardest part was earning enough money. I had to earn at least $1500. That's a lot of money for a kid my age. We did a lot of fundraising. Personally it was hard for me to ask people for money. I couldn't do it very well. I called and emailed my relatives and friends, and I was so happy when most of them donated. Every little bit helped. As a group we did a lot of fundraisers. We had a coin drive, sold shin guard sleeves/wristbands, sold soccer balls, held a soccer clinic for little kids, and even worked a night at Texas Roadhouse. It was a lot of fun working there. We got to dance and talk and just have fun. It was great.

Tabitha

One of the hardest parts of preparing for the trip was raising the money to get there. We were constantly trying to squeeze fundraising into our already crazy schedules. Between soccer practices, games, school, parents working, homework, chores, church activities, and whatever else life decided to throw at us, fitting it in was often a challenge.

It didn't matter; rain, snow, hail, or shine we were out either going door-to-door or running soccer clinics. I am so grateful, though, for everybody who donated and made it possible for me to go on this trip.

Everybody was so generous and willing to help out. I learned that people who didn't have much to begin with were so eager to give. Even little kids came running to dump the money from their piggy banks into my basket, and every little bit helped. Some days went better than others. One evening, my mother and I had been going door-to-door for about an hour in a crazy snowstorm. At half of the houses where we knocked, the people weren't home and almost everyone who was home was a child. My mom and I were both so confused as to why nobody was home. Finally, at the last door we knocked on they told us that they had a big church meeting for the adults in the neighborhood that night. Not great timing!

Maizy

Honestly, I didn't have it too bad. I had loads of help from my family, but I'd have to say fundraising took up a lot of time and was frustrating at points. For example, I did most of my fundraising online, so I could get donations from far away family.

It was difficult at some times, and easier at others. When I was out fundraising for hours in the cold, without much luck, I had to keep pushing through the storm and continue fundraising. If I backed out now, I'd be letting myself and everyone else down.

Throughout the whole process of fundraising, learning, and preparing others and myself for the trip, I learned that I like to stand up and be a leader. I did not like the feeling of being a follower, or just a tag-along. During this whole Save-A-Thon For Africa experience, I acquired a commitment to helping people in need.

I traveled to Salt Lake City with some other girls who were going, and we handed out bagged lunches and other necessities to the homeless. They were so grateful for one little peanut-butter-and-jelly sandwich. It really made me think about how greedy we can be sometimes and how easily disappointed we can be when we don't get something new.

Noheli

The hardest thing for me was raising the money because I had to door to door knocking the whole time. I had doors slammed in my face a lot of times and I met dead ends. If I didn't get enough money the first day, I had to work longer the next day. I learned that I could communicate with other people better than before the trip. What I learned about others was when we needed help, people stepped forward to help us.

They didn't just think about themselves, and I thought that was very neat.

It was pretty hard for me to commit to the trip because sometimes I didn't want to go knocking, but I thank my dad for pushing me to go.

Some people thought it was just a joke because no ordinary girl goes up to their door and says they are going to Africa, so it was hard to explain that it was for real.

Alex

Raising all the money, and getting on the plane to Africa was never hard, it was so exciting and thrilling.

TAKING OFF

Wednesday, March 21

Adam

It's amazing how fast time goes by when you are working hard and preparing for an ambitious journey. With funds raised, passports in hand, vaccinations received, and bags packed, it was time to go. We were all experiencing similar feelings like the anxious moments and jitters before the opening kickoff of a soccer game as we boarded our flights on Wednesday, March 26, 2014, and so began the "no-turning back" phase of the adventure.

Kylie

As I'm sitting in the San Francisco Airport with my soccer team on our layover, I'm thinking about how crazy this idea that my dad, Dickson, and I have come up with and how well it's all coming together. I never would have thought that this would all actually be happening. I mean, how many young, American soccer players get to travel almost eight thousand miles to Africa with their best friends to play an international match against local Nigerian soccer teams? It's crazy! I'm so excited to see these girls' reactions to a different culture and have the adventure of their lives. Less than twenty-four hours until we finally arrive in Lagos!

Alex

Once we were at the Houston airport waiting for our plane to depart to Lagos, we were the only white people in our terminal. And you could tell that everyone was so surprised to see a whole bunch of white people getting on a plane to Africa. Everyone was staring at us and whispering to their neighbors. You could tell that it was out of the ordinary, and it definitely felt like it was.

Britnee

The thought of being in Africa in about twenty-four hours didn't seem real! It feels like a dream to me still. The day on planes was really long, with long layovers, but what made it worth it was to think we would be in Nigeria soon. The flight from Houston to Africa was the worst one.

I've never been on a plane for twelve hours straight before! I was in the middle of Hailey and Chris and I couldn't sleep at all. They had nice televisions in front of every seat, but I still got restless. We were the only white people on the plane. I slept on the floor of the plane; it was actually pretty comfortable. At one point my feet were out in the aisle and one of the flight attendants tripped over them. She got down on her hands and knees to see if there really was a person on the ground. The plane was dark, and all the lights were off because it was in the middle of the night. Chris took a pillow and covered me, and she moved on. It was pretty funny.

Bizzy

On the first day of our adventure we left at 3:30AM to head to the Salt Lake City Airport. After about an hour and twenty minutes of flying, we have now arrived safely in the San Francisco Airport. We waited for our next flight, which would take us to Houston, Texas. I was super excited! And everyone was safe and everything had gone well.

In Houston, while we were waiting for our plane to Lagos, we played soccer with a little girl and a little British boy. We gave them each soccer balls.

Our plane to Nigeria was very nice! It was a Boeing 787 Dreamliner and I actually had a very good time. The twelve or more hours we had to fly went by surprisingly fast. I never got plane sick. We watched movies and slept the whole way.

Hanna

Before we got on the bus to go to the Salt Lake City Airport, some of us went to Subway for a midnight snack. This trip was my first time flying. It was kind of scary but fun. I didn't get sick at all. But I think it was mostly because I slept the whole time. The first flight, from Salt Lake to San Francisco, was only two hours. So that one was not bad. The second flight from San Francisco to Houston was about four hours, so it wasn't bad either. The final flight to Lagos was very long, but I was able to sleep most of the time. There were movies to watch, so that made it go by fast.

Hailey

When we got to the airport I was shivering and really cold and nervous.

We went through security quickly and smoothly and we eventually got on the plane. The first flight I sat by my sister Elizabeth, and lucky me, I was sleepy so I slept the whole time! When we got to Houston, it was rainy and we had a five-hour layover. That layover actually went by very quickly. Then as it became time to board our flight to Lagos, I noticed how few white people were actually waiting to board our flight. It didn't shock me and I thought it was cool!

I was tired and nervous, and I just wanted the plane ride to be over with. Britnee and I watched the movie Taken 2, and then I got really tired and started dozing off. I woke up a couple of times because Britnee kept pushing on the bottom of my seat since she tried to sleep on the floor of the plane! HA! But it was okay. I was comfortable and everything was good! I slept the rest of the flight and woke up with about an hour and a half left. I was very drowsy, and I had really bad jet lag.

ON THE GROUND

Thursday, March 27

Adam

The journey just to get to Nigeria was long and difficult. We left Utah around 3AM Wednesday morning and by the time we landed in Lagos it was 8 AM *Thursday* morning, March 27 in Utah. The trip was a total of 29 hours of travel time. This was the longest trip any of the girls had ever taken and for some, their first time flying – ever. The effort and energy combined with uncertainty and fear of the unknown would definitely take a toll. When you consider how you feel after sitting for so long, being tired, eating food at 40,000 feet altitude, and knowing you are going somewhere you have been told can be dangerous, the emotions and thoughts you have can be overwhelming. You feel sort of foggy and almost like you are in a dream.

Maizy

What I underestimated most of all was the heat and humidity. Once we walked out of the pleasant, air-conditioned airplane, and into the airport, I knew there wasn't going to be a non-sweaty time the whole week. It was like walking into a sauna turned on high! Also, I thought it would be cleaner. Yet again, I was wrong. The Lagos Airport was run down and very dirty.

Once we got outside, I assumed I would see more poverty and disease and was taken aback by all of the well-fed children and growing businesses that took its place. Instead of sickness and poverty, I witnessed more of an organized chaos. It was crazy, yet beautiful in its own way.

On our way to our first hotel, if I looked out the window, I'd have a pair of eyes six inches away in the next car. The driving was madness! There were no stop signs or speed limits, and the honking cars were constant. What was even more insane was that there were people running through the traffic that seemed to be going 100 mph! Whenever we stopped, peddlers would come crowding around the windows trying to sell us stuff or asking for money.

Bizzy

When we landed in Nigeria, there were green trees and bushes everywhere! It literally looked like a jungle. It looked a little chilly outside so I put my jacket on and right when we got off the plane we were all just hit hard with heat and humidity. It felt like I was in a sauna. I started to sweat a lot, and the air was very humid, so it was hard to breathe. After that, we just waited in the airport a while for Dickson and our bodyguards.

We walked outside the airport and Adam insisted that we not let anyone help us with our bags. We walked in a very tight group. A man asked Adam what band we were, and we all laughed. Then we got into our little buses and drove to our hotel.

When we were in the buses, there were so many things to see; everyone was saying that we could drive all day and never get bored just looking out the window. When Maizy, Noheli, and I were in the hotel room, it was really fun until we found mold in our sheets and the power went out. But, the hotel staff changed our room so it all worked out in the end.

Hailey

When it was time to land, I remember looking out the window and seeing all the little shacks and no large buildings. When we got into the airport, the heat hit us in the face and the humidity made you feel damp and sticky. We got our luggage, and it seemed like an hour before we got to go outside, but when we did, it was a mess. We had to follow a man named Dickson, who is Adam's partner for Save-A-Thon. Dickson and Adam made it very clear that we were only to take directions from the two of them. It was nerve-wracking and hot, and everyone was in a rush. There were cars zooming past and would not stop.

We got to the vans, and they hurried and shuffled us inside. Then we started driving. The car rides were amazing and thrilling— much better than a rollercoaster. It was probably the most chaotic thing I have ever done. We actually hit someone's car and nothing happened. They kept driving, and they drove wherever they want on the road. They honked to let us know that they were close. We finally got situated at our hotel, and then we got bottled water and checked out the pool. It was beautiful compared to everything else surrounding it and everything was fine.

The smell was really strong and unpleasant and the heat and humidity did not help.

Britnee

Well, our first day here got off to a good start! It was a crazy one, too. We landed in Nigeria and from the plane window it looked like a bunch of shacks and fields. It was a cloudy day, although I expected it to be really sunny. When we got off the plane it felt like we had stepped into a sauna. It was about 95 degrees, and the humidity was worse than I have ever felt. For the first time in my life I was in the minority. It was a weird thing to have people stop and completely stare at me, and want to take "snaps," or photos, with me.

I was surprised at how many people had phones there. They aren't like our iPhones, but some had smart phones, which I didn't expect to see. Walking to the vans was the craziest experience yet. I was dragging along my two huge 50-pound suitcases and one of them fell and spilled open in the middle of the road. Tons of people swarmed over asking if they could carry my bag or if they could help, and I just had to reply, "No." The security met us at our vans where people were throwing our bags in.

One of the things that was the most shocking to see was the policemen standing just holding their huge guns. That's not something you see in America. I wonder how many times they've used their guns.

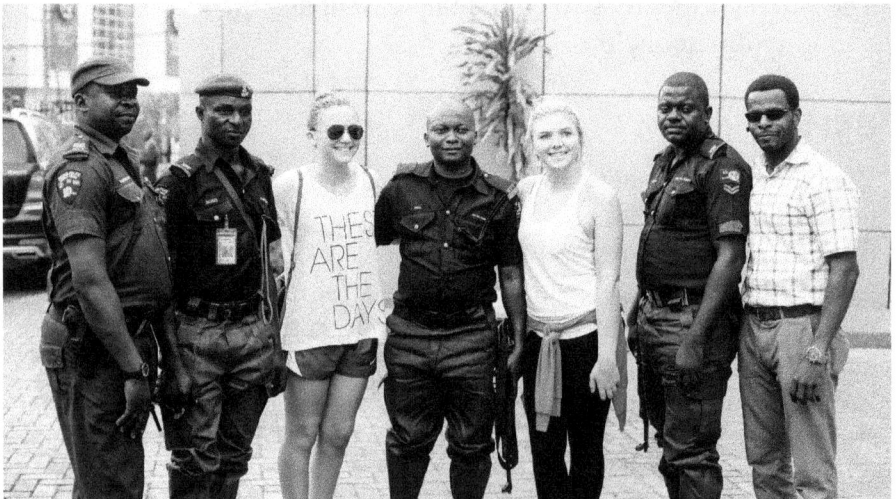

Driving to our hotel we had a ton of people run up to the van when we were stopped in traffic and beg for money or food. I figured people asking for money here wouldn't be much different than homeless people in America. The difference is that here there are a ton more, and they didn't seem to be asking for money to buy alcohol or drugs, they were asking for money to buy food, clothes, or build their house. They literally have nothing.

The car rides are one of my favorite things being here. There are no lanes on the roads, no street signs or signals, and no police cars enforcing anything. There are speed limits but nobody follows them. EVERYONE honks all the time. They honk to say they are passing you or coming through, or they honk to let you know they are coming up next to you. It's very aggressive driving. It's a completely different experience than driving in America. At one point, our driver got angry at the car in front of us and rammed into the back of it three times. The guy in the car didn't even seem that mad about it either—he had many dents in his car. People just weave between the cars in the road and come right up to your car window selling anything you could imagine.

The worst thing about Africa for me is the smell. The country itself smells bad also because they don't have a sewage system. People just leave their garbage on the sides of the road or pee on the side of their house.

Tabitha

When we first arrived in Nigeria, I was so surprised at how everyone there was so willing to help. Almost everyone was always smiling. They just wanted to talk to us or touch our skin and hair. It was so crazy to me how kind and generous everyone was. It showed what sweet hearts they all had and they were all so forgiving.

It was really hard for me though, when we were in Africa, to see the lack of respect that they had for the people living around them, especially little children. Once we were handing out bracelets and everyone stormed over. This older kid pushed down a little boy and nobody tried to help him up. They just stepped on him like he wasn't even there. Later when we went to the orphanage, the very kind lady there picked up a little boy who was just a couple months old and just had him dangling by his arm as she waited for me to come to her and hold the little boy.

Noheli

I thought that the people wouldn't be that nice to us. I also saw a lot of trees and cars I honestly thought there wouldn't be a lot of cars. There was also a Cold Stone Creamery, which I thought was crazy.

Adam

After the long, long journey to Nigeria we all settled into the hotel for some sleep. But since Utah is seven hours behind Nigeria even though your body is exhausted and it's bedtime in Nigeria it can be difficult to get to sleep. That's called jet lag and you really don't understand it until you've experienced it. This next account by Britnee is a great reminder what jet lag can do to your mind and what the deadbolt is for.

Britnee

On our first morning in Africa, Hailey and I were woken up by a scary experience. Due to jet lag it felt like it was four in the morning when we heard a knock on our door. A voice we didn't recognize came with it: "Housekeeping." Neither of us moved. Then the knock came again.

Hailey shook me awake and told me to go get the door. We were so confused and scared as to why housekeeping was knocking at our door at four in the morning. I started walking to the door when I heard it open and footsteps coming in.

I started screaming "NO! Leave! Please leave!" terrified that this man wanted to hurt us.

When I heard the door shut I opened it half an inch and there was the poor housekeeping guy looking so confused as to why we were screaming. He asked to clean our room and I told him to come back when it wasn't four in the morning. He looked so confused and left. Then Hailey checked her phone and it was 10:30 am…so that was our first experience with jet lag!

That morning, we had some time and decided to go to a soccer field,which was more like a dirt field, and kick a soccer ball around. What we saw there was amazing. Hundreds of school kids in their uniforms from different schools were playing soccer with garbage they found onthe ground. When we got out of the van, we really felt like celebrities. Everyone stopped and ran over as we got in a circle and started passing a ball to them. They showed us their amazing tricks.

One thing I noticed was that only the boys were playing, the girls were standing off in their own circle. We went over and asked them why they weren't playing, and they told us they weren't allowed. This made me really sad and made me aware of the reason I was there: to show these girls that they are just as valuable as boys and they can play if they want too. One of the kids had a little box playing music. So, we all got in a circle with them and started dancing. We handed out some bracelets and were amazed at how they fought over them.

Kaycee

Today we went to a park in Lagos. There were a lot of kids there and I was excited but also nervous about playing and interacting with them. When we got out of the vans and started playing it was a lot of fun. The kids were really good, and I loved seeing their smiles and how happy they were to play soccer. It makes me so happy just seeing them smile. It was so much fun and I didn't want to leave.

Bizzy

On our first full day we decided to go to a dirt soccer field and play some soccer. When we got there, everyone was staring at us because we were white. I never saw any other white people during our entire trip, so I guess that's why they were staring, but it was just amazing how they walked over and just started playing soccer with us. They were so kind and had the coolest names. Some of the girls got in a group and danced with us. I was so sad when we had to leave them!

Hanna

We slept until noon. A little while later, all the girls went swimming. Then the adults got us Dominos Pizza! They actually had one here! And a Cold Stone Creamery! I didn't think they'd have anything like that. Then we all went to the soccer field and played soccer with the little kids. We all got in a juggling circle and passed and juggled. Let me tell you... they are all so adorable. They're all amazing at football. They were trying to teach us their skills... yeah, we failed. It was so fun though. Then we went back and everyone was pushing everyone into the pool (mostly my dad was the one pushing). Later we went to Cold Stone. It was lots of fun. I got cookie dough but I don't think it was really cookie dough.

Hailey

Our hotel room is clean and pretty nice. We wash our faces with bottled water because the water out of the tap is making me break out and smells like metal. We haven't showered and my hair is a grease ball and we really stink. We made oatmeal in our room for breakfast then went to the lobby to load the vans so we could go play soccer with some kids at a local school.

When we drive past all the people they just stare at you and you just wave and then they get really excited and overjoyed. They always do the "thumbs up" and it's adorable. Once we got to the field the kids just stared at us wondering who we were and why we were there. We played soccer and handed out bracelets and soccer balls. One of the girls complimented me on my earrings and I told her if she would dance for me I would give them to her. So, she did and I had to give them away. In order to not make a scene, I slowly slipped the earrings into her hand.

We played soccer for a little while more and it felt amazing to see so much random skill that they had learned all on their own. The girls loved us and wanted so many "snaps" or pictures. When we left we saw them videoing us and it was hard to say goodbye. When we got back to the hotel around 3PM we fell asleep again because we were so tired.

We mostly just relaxed and tried to get rid of our horrible jet lag! It was a nice rest day!

Adam

Alex, the only college student in our group, had a weekly class she absolutely could not miss. This class fell on a Wednesday, which was the day we were scheduled to leave. So, after much juggling we arranged for her to fly the day after the larger group left. Due to the security concerns of having her travel alone, and totally committed to her not missing the trip, we arranged to have her aunt, our photographer, and my older daughter, Marissa, fly with her. It worked out great and we were so fortunate to have Alex with us. It was also fortunate that our photographer, Travis, had been through the airport arrival process in Lagos a month earlier with me so he knew the ropes. Generally not something you want to try on your own.

By the way, the day we arrived back in Utah, the next Wednesday, she went straight to that same class. Talk about a committed college student!

Alex

Once we conquered the 11.5-hour flight to Lagos, the most amazing journey of my life began. As soon as we stepped off the airplane, it was a completely different atmosphere and culture; it was absolutely incredible. Everywhere we went, I was looking all around me, amazed at how the airport worked, how unbelievably hot it was, and how nice the people were. As we were walking to go get our bags a man grabbed my hair and was like "I love you white hair." It was so different for them to see. You could tell that they were all a little skeptical about us as we walked through the airport. When we were getting our bags checked they said, "They are heavy, why?" and we would tell them it was our food and clothes, and they opened up all our bags and asked what each of the things in there was.

As soon as we got through all that, we saw my Dad, sister, Adam, Kylie and Dickson there waiting for us. As soon as we got to them Adam's first words were "Okay, walk fast, and stick close." I think that that was the only time I got a little nervous throughout the whole trip. When we began to walk we kept getting cut off and shoved around because everyone knows where they want to go, and they don't allow anyone to get in their way.

When we walked out of the airport, it was incredible. Nothing like I ever imagined. Cars EVERYWHERE, people EVERYWHERE, just sitting and staring; most with no shoes, sitting on the railings on the sides of the roads.

Literally everywhere. When we got to our van, I remember seeing three rather large African men standing with very big guns in their hands, all for our protection. The car ride was like a carnival ride. Haha! I loved every second of it. I remember my Dad turning to me and saying, "Hold on tight." He was being serious. It was insane: everyone was honking, no such thing as actual lanes of traffic, no blinkers, no stop signs or stop lights, people lining the sides of the roads, people in

between the so called "lanes of traffic" trying to sell things, cars trying to squeeze in a space that they shouldn't try to squeeze into.

All the women walking down the streets had baskets on top of their head with a large load - their necks would have to be very, very strong. There were street markets everywhere. I wanted to get out and just walk down the streets. It looked so cool and so authentic. And EVERYONE, as soon as they saw that there was a whole bunch of white people in the car, was smiling and waving and saying "hi." It was then that I realized that these people, who the news and the world make out to be rude and very scary people, were some of the most sincere, nicest and most beautiful people I had ever met, that was not the only time that I realized that.

Driving down the streets of Lagos I was amazed at how busy and hectic it was. The scenery and colors of the buildings and rocks were all so pretty. It was all orange, brown, pink, teal, and yellow, and all the buildings had a flat rooftop. The people, as I said before, were everywhere; it was like a parade was going on. It was so busy, constantly. As we were driving down the street we saw Cold Stone and Dominos, and for some reason I thought that was so odd, haha that was me just thinking it was poor little Africa, but it isn't "poor little Africa." It is a country just like ours, with food, just like ours, with great people and an amazing culture.

When we arrived at our hotel, I was in shock. It was absolutely beautiful: a gated entrance, cream and orange architecture, guards everywhere, and all of the workers were so inviting and excited to have us there. The pool was so pretty, and the mural on the wall was absolutely beautiful—I wanted to take it home with me and put it in my room.

There were lizards crawling all over the floors, which was bad because I really hate anything that is in the reptile category. But I figured they were from Africa, and they were going to be about the only wildlife I was going to be able to see, so I was okay with it. At night we got on top of the roof of the hotel. It was no doubt the most beautiful thing I have ever seen. It was breathtaking. I never wanted to leave. You could see all the little nooks and corners of Lagos, the lights, the buildings, the street markets, the people dancing everywhere, and the honking still going on; it was so pretty. Still to this day, a whole month later, I cannot get that picture out of my head. I am sure that I will say this over and over again throughout this journal, but it is safe to say that Africa is the most beautiful place I have ever seen. As I said in my journal that I kept the whole time while in Africa on my first night, "This place is so amazing in every way possible, I don't ever want to go home."

Around 9:00 that night we took the whole group and our guards to Cold Stone. It was down the street a bit in the dark. Adam told us

before we left to not be loud and to stick together. Walking down the streets of Lagos was such a thrill. You had to be looking down and up at the same time or you would run into a person or step in a hole. The sidewalk was not really a sidewalk: it was a bunch of slabs of wood, cement rocks, concrete, and gravel with holes everywhere. The people, even at nine o'clock at night, were everywhere. I remember walking down the road, and it was pretty dark, and this man pops out of a corner out of nowhere and got so close to my face and just said "Hi." He was so nice, but he also really scared me. It was pretty crazy. Because if you got too far into the road, you would get run over and I found that if a car honks it means in a "polite" way, move!

Once we got to Cold Stone, I could tell that everyone was so intrigued that there were twenty white people just sitting there eating ice cream, but they were all so nice. I remember the workers singing us some kind of song as we were about to leave, and that was pretty cool.

THE JOURNEY TO OSUN

Saturday, March 29

Adam

Now that the entire team was in the country we were ready to travel to Osun State. I have taken this trip multiple times and as unpleasant as the journey is, disastrous roads, terrible traffic, and crazy drivers, the four-six hour journey is really quite entertaining. I wondered how the girls would do traveling and kept my fingers crossed that the girls and adults wouldn't get car sick or have to stop to use the bathroom since I knew a "bathroom" in Nigeria is a far cry from the worst rest-stop bathroom we have in America.

We made it safely to Osun and the adventure really got going.

Britnee

Last night Hailey and I suffered from really bad jet lag and only slept one hour. We left at 5AM when it was still dark out to drive to Osun. It ended up being about a six-hour drive because of the insane driving. At one point our driver decided the road he was on was too busy, so he and a bunch of other cars drove through the barrier separating the two directions of highway and drove on the road into **oncoming** traffic. After about an hour or so of driving on the

wrong side of the road we ran into a traffic jam that was absolute chaos. The oncoming traffic came to a stop and ran into the cars like our car, which had crossed onto that road because it was less busy. I remember thinking to myself that it was common sense that this was going to happen. After waiting in this traffic jam for about a half hour, Dickson and his guys got out and moved one of the cement barriers and started directing traffic so we could cross back to the right side of the road.

When we finally arrived at Osun we got settled in our villa at the Zenababs Half Moon Resort. It was such a beautiful place and it made me realize how beautiful Africa is! Everything was very green, and not altered by big industrial buildings. The manager of the resort was especially accommodating, and he did everything he could for us.

Kaycee

On Saturday we drove from Lagos to Osun. We stopped at a government building and talked to the governor's assistant about the kids in Nigeria and how little they have. He gave us an inspirational speech.

He said, "The only word that can cure all hate is love." I truly believe this and hope that we can all learn to be more loving.

Bizzy

We rode in little buses to Osun where the driving there is crazy! Cars are literally inches away from other cars. And they don't have blinkers, stop signs, lanes, or stoplights! They just use their horns. It was exciting to drive four hours from Lagos to Osun. We looked out the window the whole time. I remember I could barely keep my eyes open I was so tired but I didn't want to fall asleep because there was so much to see.

In Osun we stayed in the cutest little dorms that had little bugs on the walls. By this point in the trip we were so used to them that I started to ignore them, which I would not have done in my own home in Utah.

Hailey

We woke up early today and I was really hungry and tired. We were on our way to Osun state, which is considered the most peaceful place in the whole country. We drove for four hours on a very bumpy road. I was nervous again and sometimes we would go on the whole other side of the median and cross in between the two highways into oncoming traffic. It seemed like there was no way out of the crazy traffic. Finally, the police, who were with us, had to move the concrete median and allow a way for the cars going to Osun to get through. The drive was really long, and my legs were cramped. It was amazing to see how crazy the drivers were and

how they don't have any driving laws at all. If they do have laws the drivers certainly don't follow them because at one point we were going 125 MPH I am pretty sure that's the fastest I have ever driven inside a car.

I later learned from Adam while it might have felt like 125 MPH, it was actually 125 Kilometers Per Hour, or about 75 MPH.

Once we arrived at the hotel, it was beautiful. All of the people were especially nice and the owner Sesan was so friendly and kind; he donated water to us, let us ride a donkey, pet an ostrich, and ride in his paddle boats even though they were infested with spiders.

The hotel had a nice pool and lobby. We slept in a hut type of structure, but there were a lot of bugs and spiders and ants on the walls and in the showers and sink. At night I was afraid I had bugs crawling on me and bed bugs in my hair but I just had to keep in mind that it was Africa not America and it wasn't going to be easy. Fortunately, we had air conditioning, a shower, a refrigerator and a bed that was hard as a rock but it was a bed and it worked and I was alive.

SOCCER CLINIC

Adam

The clinic was the part when we all started to really engage with the kids there. To watch these Nigerian kids and these amazing American young women engage with each other through their favorite sport was surreal for me. To see this beautiful sight made me indescribably happy and made the hundreds of hours, the thousands of dollars, and the tens of thousands of airline miles I spent all worth it. This is also when I think the girls started to see the beauty of this whole effort as the walls of race, gender, nationality, and language came down.

Alex

After we all settled in, we headed to the soccer clinic that we were holding. When we got to the field it was more than I could have ever dreamed of. There was a big stereo and speakers playing music and SO many kids waiting for us, most without shoes, or with just one cleat on, and in jean shorts. It was absolutely incredible to see.

They were so excited to see us and when we told them what to do they did exactly what we asked of them. It was very fun to play soccer with all of the kids; they were amazing.

I remember a game of "head-catch" when I was the one throwing the ball. A lot of the boys would get out, and they would cheat and sneak back into the game. The teachers would yell at them about having honor and integrity. It was incredible to see the values that they were teaching these kids. They were all so kind and happy, and so willing to help. After a while some of the women who were helping us on Adam's team gave us some bottled water. Then the kids fought over the water like they hadn't had water all day, and they probably hadn't. I remember just putting my water down and not drinking it and they all just kind of looked at me strangely, like I was wasting their valued water.

They loved to take pictures with us, "snaps" as they call them. Everyone would come and ask us if they could have a snap with us, and once I took a photo, they all wanted to see it.

I also noticed in their culture that for girls to play soccer wasn't really accepted. The boys were especially mean to the girls. I remember one time I was shooting around with some of the kids both boys and girls, and they asked me to shoot on their goalie. I remember placing a rather nice shot into the upper corner and they all looked at me in amazement. They couldn't believe a young woman like myself could be good at soccer. I could tell that they really idolized all of us.

All the kids really wanted something of ours to have. I couldn't tell you how many times people asked for my "soccer boots," jewelry, shin guards, or my socks. It was sad to see how badly they wanted them. As soon as we started giving away bracelets everyone started coming our way and asking for one.

I also noticed that to get each other's attention they made a kissing noise and somehow they knew exactly who they were talking to, the girls on Adam's team who were helping out laughed at all of us when we tried to do it.

The coolest part of the whole trip was right after Adam announced the Bridges Cup and how some of the kids were going to have the opportunity to come to the United States for a week. I was sitting next to a boy when Adam told them, and I remember him looking at me and tapping me on the shoulder, and saying, "Is he being serious? It has always been my dream to come to America."

I told him yes! "Some of you will be coming to America to play soccer for a week and some may even get a college scholarship."

And I remember him looking at me and he said with tears in his eyes, "Wow that is really cool. I hope they pick me." It broke my heart; it was so incredible.

At the end of the clinic there were water bags and garbage everywhere. Adam and Dickson told all of the kids through the microphone to go and pick up one piece of garbage and throw it away and then they would get a prize. The kids looked at us and asked, "What is garbage?" After we explained, they all went and picked up a piece and brought it back. The prize was a bag full of dinner and water for the night. It was amazing to see how happy they were to receive the food.

It was heartbreaking to see the trials that they endure on a daily basis, and even more so when I compared them to my daily life. It was touching to be able to see how blessed I am, and hard to see how much I take for granted. It truly changed my life to see the way that these kids live their lives.

I spoke to another young boy and asked him about his life and how old he was. He was eighteen, my age. His family was homeless, and he had two little sisters. His father had been killed a couple months before. He told me that his mom was in bad condition, and that he always wanted to go to school just for her. My eyes watered as he told me this story. I looked away so that he didn't know that I was crying. It was the most heartbreaking story that I had ever heard; yet this young man had so much strength and devotion for his family. He, an eighteen-year-old African boy, changed my life.

When we got back to Zenababs, Sesan, the Resort Manager, made us all an ostrich burger for dinner with a kind of bread that was very sweet and thick. At first, the idea of eating an ostrich burger was quite disturbing, but it was actually pretty tasty.

Britnee

We were two hours late to the soccer clinic because our bus took forever. That's Africa time for you. They don't seem to understand the importance of being on time.

Each of us was in charge of an area of the soccer field, and we were in charge of organizing a drill to do with rotating groups. Mine was a 1v1 drill to a water bottle since they didn't have cones and there was plenty of trash lying around.

It was amazing to me how serious these kids took the drills even though they had probably never been to something like this before.

59

It made me sad to see how much potential these amazing kids have with little room to do anything with it. That's why I love the idea of Bridges To America helping these kids make something of their talents and their lives. Each competition was like life or death to these kids because it was their one chance to stand out at something they are good at.

We told them that the winning boys and girls teams of the Bridges Cup will get to go to America. When we said this, a few started to cry and kept asking us, "We would get to go to America?" It made me realize how blessed I am to live in a place so many people dream of. I'm excited to see what the Cup brings.

Some of the kids would kick the soccer balls into the bushes so they could get them later. It made me sad that the culture in Africa teaches the kids that everyone is on his or her own, and that cheating was the way for them to get what they wanted or needed. That moral character seemed to create many of the problems that Africa has right now. But how do we change a whole culture or country's mindset?

It was heart breaking to see the trials that they endure on a daily basis, and even more so when I compared them to my daily life. It was touching to be able to see how blessed I am, and hard to see how much I take for granted. It truly changed my life to see the way that these kids live their lives.

Kaycee

Later in the day, we held a soccer clinic for some of the kids in the village. Most of them were my age or older. It was hard at first to coach them because they were older and it was kind of awkward. But I learned to just be myself and then they respected me and would interact with me more easily. Once we all started playing, it was a lot of fun.

The boys were fun to play with in small groups. We talked and danced and passed the soccer balls around.

This clinic really opened my eyes to how good I have it in the United States. Most kids didn't have cleats and many didn't have shoes or shin guards. It was so sad because they all asked me where

I got my "boots." They wanted my boots and my soccer ball but I couldn't give them away. It broke my heart.

Megan

We are just finishing our third day of the Utah to Nigeria trip and we finally got to interact with the Nigerian kids in Osun by holding a soccer clinic and teaching them some of what we know and how we practice in the US.

I was so excited all day for this clinic and the moment was finally here. When it came time to load everything into the bus we all got our gear on and met outside our rooms.

There was no sign of the bus. Over an hour later the bus finally arrived, making us extremely late for our own clinic that we had planned and were supposed to run. The driver told us it took longer than he expected because he was worried that we would be too hot. He wanted to wait for the day to cool down. By the time we arrived, we were very late and it was still incredibly hot. There were over one hundred and fifty Nigerian kids waiting for us. It was amazing to see that so many kids showed up to have a group of American teenage girls teach them a few soccer skills.

We climbed out of the bus and got started immediately. We just thought we would show them some of the basics of soccer. I was assigned to work with my dad on a couple of shooting drills. Whenever we stopped to speak to them or to give them a tip, they immediately turned their attention to us and listened with full intent, even though they were one thousand times better than we were at things like juggling. I was surprised how few girls showed up to train with us.

I was distraught because even when we went to visit a schoolyard the girls said they couldn't play. When the group of girls at the clinic moved to my station with my dad I instantly fell in love with them because of how strong they were and how willing they were to learn the game of soccer. I admired their strength and resilience and hoped they learned from the clinic that girls can do ANYTHING boys can. In fact, girls can do anything they want. I really hoped they would keep playing soccer as an example that if they set their minds to a goal they could accomplish anything they desired.

I was asked to take picture after picture with the kids. I really didn't mind because it made me feel famous. The people were incredible. I began to fall deeper in love with their culture and wanted to stay even longer. I was anxious and excited for the next day when we would visit the orphanages.

Bizzy

The soccer clinic was such a great experience. I really enjoyed teaching the kids some of the rules of soccer. Even though I was teaching I also learned a lot from them, too.

The kids kept asking me for my cleats, but we had a soccer game and I needed them for that.

Hanna

Running the soccer camp for over one hundred and forty Nigerian kidswas fun, hard, and kind of scary. Many of our team members made rubber band bracelets to give to the kids. As soon as the kids saw them, they all dived for them while they were still on our wrists. The kids all really wanted them and we didn't have enough for everyone so they took them off our wrists.

It was a little bit intimidating because we were expected to teach soccer to twelve to eighteen year-old kids who played "futbol" all day, every day. We showed them some techniques and taught them some rules of the game, but they taught us through their own skills. It was a lot more fun to juggle with them because they were so good!

Hailey

When we got to the soccer clinic, they all gathered closer to our bus. We quickly started warming up and then split up into six groups for fifteen minutes each. My assignment was to teach a 3v3 drill, which is complicated to explain to African boys who don't speak English very well or none at all. A local man came to help my sister and me so they would actually understand, but it was very frustrating to run it on our own without much help. I was amazed to see all of the talent that these kids had playing in their bare feet. It was a great learning experience.

We played two games. First, we played "head-catch" and they took it so seriously. Most of the boys in my group were disappointed because they didn't get chosen to be in the finals. The second game was a simple shoot-out which was also taken seriously. The kids who got out first came over at once and started filming us, taking pictures of us and touching our hair; it was odd and kind of cool at the same time.

Afterwards, we handed them bags with a shirt inside and some food. Many of the kids asked me for my cleats but I never gave them away. It broke my heart seeing that most of the kids played in their bare feet. Some kids started kicking our soccer balls over the fence so they could go get them later and keep them. We took so many pictures, and they loved us so much they didn't want us to go. Finally, Dickson told all of us that it was time to go.

DAY OF SERVICE

Sunday, March 30

Adam

The entire trip was really about service but Sunday in this very religious country, about evenly split 50% Christian and 50% Muslim, took on particular meaning as we spent a very full day serving. It is not hyperbole to say that on this day our team touched many lives and had our hearts changed forever as we saw things and had chances to help others that few people ever get. Interestingly it was our longest and most varied day of the trip. Service is hard work but the rewards from doing so are boundless. I loved this day as the true benefits of our venture in Nigeria became crystal clear.

CHURCH

Alex

Day 4, Sunday, was absolutely incredible. We started the day off by waking up early and making our way to the Church of Jesus Christ of Latter Day Saints chapel. It took us quite awhile to find the church, but Dickson was very determined to get us there. On our way to the church we got in a traffic jam, and it was hilarious. We were in a van owned by the State so people were supposed to get out of our way.

At least that's how our drivers drove. They would turn into oncoming traffic and a car would be coming straight into us. The cars wouldn't stop and kept coming right for us. Our driver, Dickson and many of our body guards got out of the vehicles and were screaming and fighting with a man who nearly ran into our van. I think his brakes were bad and he couldn't stop in time. After a while, Dickson had enough and just started pushing the car backwards out of our way. We finally made it to the church.

It was in a cement building, not in very good shape. There was the traditional sign on the front of the church, and once we stepped inside the building with no doors, or windows, but with holes for them, it looked like an abandoned building. We then walked up some very steep stairs and went into a room where there were at least fifteen to twenty other Africans attending the main meeting called Sacrament Meeting.

We walked in right after the sacrament was passed and this experience was truly amazing. I was crying the whole time. It was so touching to be able to see how much people love the same gospel we live thousands of miles away and how proud these people were to have it in their lives.

When we walked in, we could see how delighted they were to have us there. Hailey, Britnee, and I were sitting in the very front of the room, where the branch president (the local leader) and his counselors would usually sit. It was so cool and truly inspiring to be able to look out at all these people and see the true glow in their eyes, and the love that they had for the gospel.

For the closing song we sang, "When There"s Love At Home" and the Africans sang their hearts out with no piano and a little offtune, but very, very loud. I was crying through the whole song. It was so touching to be able to unite and sing that song together.

Afterwards we went to the meeting for young women. There were only three girls who attended the class. While in this meeting the room for the Primary (kids under twelve years old) was right across the hall and you could hear them sing "I'm a member of The Church of Jesus Christ of Latter Day Saints" over and over and over again; but just that one sentence. Once again, they are SOOOOOO happy. I can't even comprehend how they can live the lives that they live and still be so happy. I kept telling myself that it is because they don't know any better, which is so sad and breaks my heart. The leader of the young women group was not much older than I. She was very skinny, very pretty, and very outgoing.

She had graduated from college and had a baby. When we went around and introduced ourselves she saw my CTR (Choose The Right) ring which is a very simple ring nearly every kid growing up in our church gets as a reminder to Choose The Right. She looked at me and said, "Can I please have this? I have always wanted one."

I have never seen someone so excited to get a CTR ring. It was so cool to be able to share that with her. She was so proud of it, and loved to flaunt it to everyone. Going to church in Africa was such an incredible experience not only spiritually, but it changed my perspective in life.

Britnee

This morning we woke up and went to Church. It made us cry when they started singing, "Because I Have Been Given Much."

These people literally have nothing and they were singing about how they need to give more to others.

Amazing! It was crazy to me that these people sacrifice eight hours to drive to their temple to worship every month or so. I was also surprised at how many churches there were. There was one right below us and right next to the one we were in. You could hear them singing their hymns very loudly and when we sang ours it was like a competition to see which church could sing the loudest. They wanted to take tons of pictures with us afterwards.

Kaycee

The people at church were so kind and welcoming. We showed up late because we couldn't find it. Everyone was loving, kind, and happy to see us. I sat next to the branch president and he was so sweet. He asked me a lot of questions but his accent was so thick I couldn't understand him. So he pulled out a piece of paper and wrote it down for me. He wrote, "I would like to introduce you." I smiled and said, "Okay, great." He asked me if we were members of the church. I said, "Yes."

He asked me who our leader was and I said, "Adam Miles."

After a woman's beautiful talk, he stood up and introduced us and asked Adam to share his testimony and feelings about being in church that day. Adam did a great job. One of the young women invited us to stay after sacrament meeting for the young women's meeting. The two girls' names were Elizabeth and Beatrice. The teacher was Agunda. They were all so sweet and beautiful when they smiled and laughed. They lit up the whole room. We talked about spiritual gifts. I learned a lot from both Beatrice and Agunda who were both funny and kind. They taught me that the ability to make people smile, or even love is a spiritual gift and that's so true.

When we all left, it was fun to get pictures with all the beautifully dressed women and the nice men. The trip to the church helped me see that we are so blessed. We have a lot of things that are easy in our lives back in the United States, yet we think our lives are so hard. But for many of the Nigerian people we met, nothing is easy. But they are all still so happy and optimistic. We all learned a lot from them.

Megan

Today was an incredible day. By far the best, sweetest, saddest and most touching day of my life by far... and I am not saying that lightly.

By the time we found the church there was only about twenty

minutes left in sacrament meeting. We all walked in late and everyone looked incredibly shocked to see a bunch of white people walking in. They helped us find seats and continued on with their meeting. The talks were great, but the best part of the whole thing was when we sang the closing hymn. They all sang so loud and strong that the wonderful feeling in the room was overwhelming. I cried more than I sang.

Bizzy

We had an amazing opportunity to go to church there. When we walked in everyone gave up their chairs for us and they sang their songs with so much spirit it made my sister cry. Then we went to the class for young women where we learned about faith and played a game that's called "Master Master Master." The church teachers were so funny and kind; it was just wonderful.

Hailey

At church it amazed me how I couldn't even understand the speakers yet I could see how strongly they believed what they were saying just by listening to the ways they spoke, and I could see in their eyes. I started crying when they sang the hymn "Love At Home."

In the young women's meeting, our leader was such a happy woman. She told me I had a strong smile and my laugh was explosive. I felt overjoyed to hear that from someone I had just met. I loved it, and I loved getting to know the people of my same faith and seeing how similar we really are.

ORPHANAGES

Alex

After we went to church we visited an orphanage. It was another incredible experience. I remember getting out of the van and

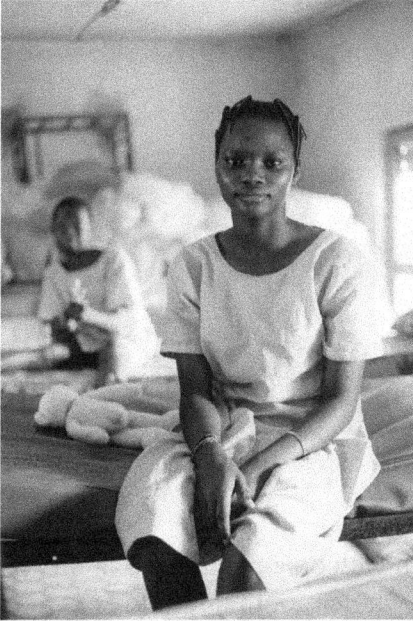

walking into the orphanage. Off to the left of us was a graveled walkway down a hill, and it overlooked what looked like another village with a lot of plants. It was breath-taking, absolutely beautiful.

As we were getting out, we saw many little kids running up the hill, and I instantly started tearing up. None of them had shoes on and they all looked really dirty, skinny, and not fed, and probably very thirsty, but yet all had huge smiles on their faces.

These kids weren't even part of the orphanage that we were about to go into, and I was already in tears.

As we walked into the orphanage, we could tell that it was not in good shape; it was dirty and falling apart, and it housed so many kids ranging from a sweet little baby to a 19-year-old. Looking at all of these children and just picturing their stories and why they were there and how strong they were, made me fall apart. When we walked in they immediately pushed us into their "backyard" which was just a gravel space and it had a wood shelter in the corner, with desks and a chalk board. They were so proud of this little area, and it was falling apart.

All the kids came in and sat down by us and we talked to all of them. They were all so shy and so fun to listen to. We handed out little rubber band bracelets, and we saw the immediate twinkle in their eyes and how we had made their day brighter. These kids were some of the most strong, loyal, and loving children I will probably ever meet in my life. They were a very tight-knit group, a family through and through. They were so welcoming, and so happy to have us there.

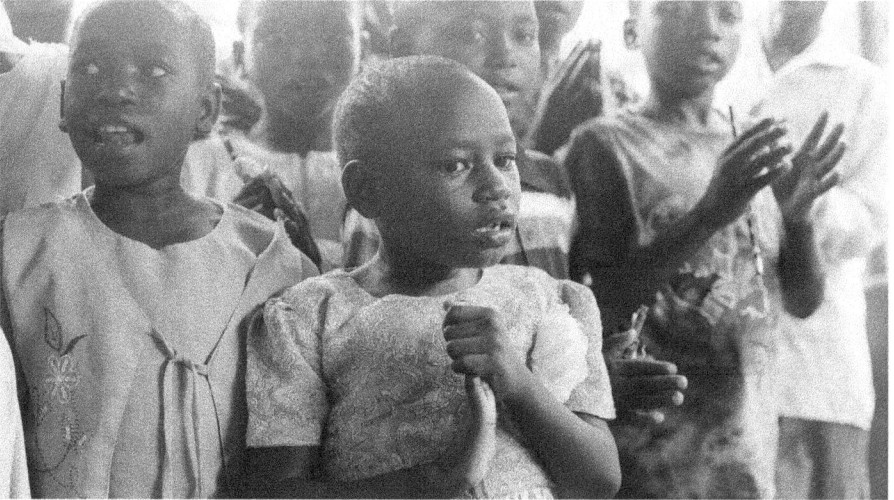

When we all sat down, they sang us a welcome song. As I sit on my bed, typing on my laptop now, a whole month later, it gives me goose bumps and makes me cry. It was the most incredible feeling that I have ever felt in my life -- to see all the smiles on the faces of these children with no mothers or fathers and to be able to clap and dance with these children that have gone through harder things than I will ever be able to comprehend, to unite as one with them, to become instant friends, and to laugh with them truly changed my life.

We listened to them sing a song, and none of us knew what they were singing. But to be a part of the experience and share the love with these children was moving. After we finished singing, the woman in charge asked us to go visit all of the children in their rooms and let them tell us their stories. Every single room was a complete cement block with dirt everywhere and very dirty foam mattresses piled in a corner where they would sleep. All of their belongings were kept on a little shelf in the other corner.

There was another single, very small room shared by at least twelve teenage boys. They all slept spooning each other because there was no room to sleep any other way. I remember one room in particular that we walked into with eight teenage girls. One of the women on Adam's team was talking to the girls about their education and their life stories.

As we sneaked in and sat on their little mattresses in the circle with these girls, I remember Omolayo talking to them about where they were from and what they were going to do with their education. The girls all told her that they were from the northeastern side of Nigeria, the dangerous side controlled by Boko Haram, and that their parents sent them to this particular school to get an education. Omolayo told us that they needed to try very, very hard in school, and to never give up. They were taught to go to church and read the Bible. They were amazing girls, and so strong and able to accomplish anything that they put their minds to.

Here I was, an 18-year-old American girl attending college at Utah State University, taking my education for granted and definitely not trying to get all that I could out of it, and being chosen to come to Africa to help the youth but more specifically the young women in Nigeria.

And I listened to their heart-wrenching stories and thought to myself that if I had their life, I probably would have given up. The fact that these girls fought so hard to get an education and poured everything that they had into it, because it's not an opportunity everyone there gets, was incredible.

I could tell that as we came in and told our stories, we were role models to them and that they looked up to us for being educated and playing soccer; two things that aren't widely accepted for women to do in Africa. It was absolutely incredible. That conversation made me want to be so much better, and made me realize how much I could do for these girls.

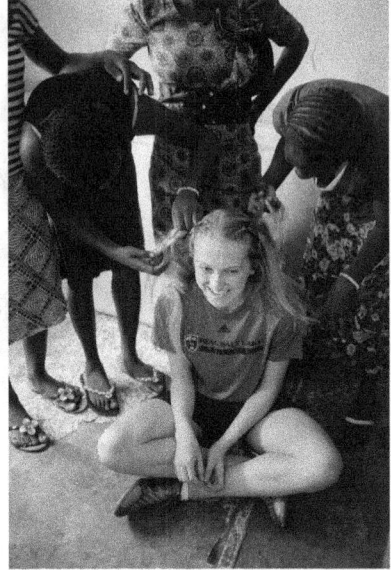

I so very badly wanted to become someone for them to look up to, someone that they could look to as their friend, someone who beat the odds, who got an education, and was a successful woman. I wanted to be that for them. I will be back someday to show those girls that hard work and dedication can pay off. I can't wait to see them again and see how they grew up and how hard they worked and that THEY, young African orphans, beat the odds and became very well- educated, young women.

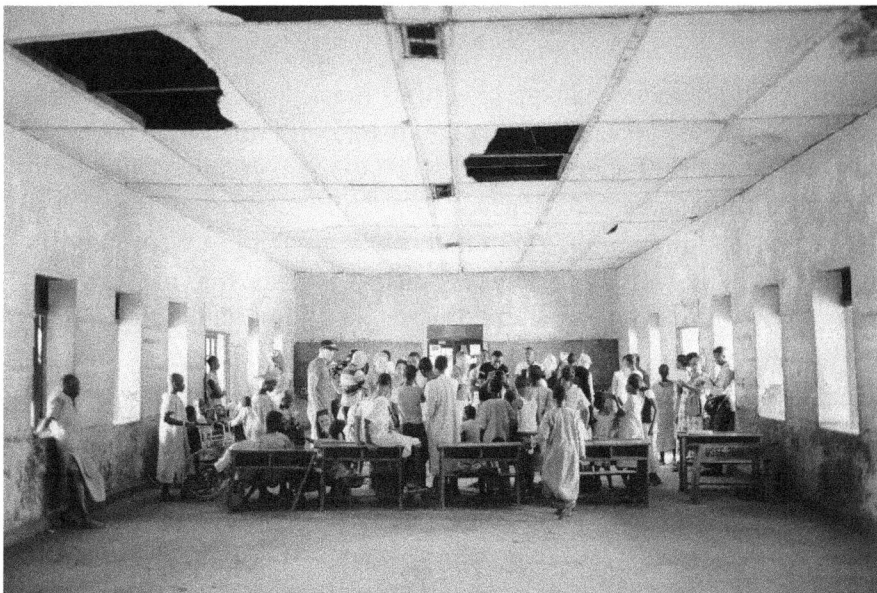

Britnee

At the orphanage for older children there were about seventy-six kids split between six rooms. That's about twelve kids to each 10x10 foot room. Their living situation was very humbling. They slept on mattresses on the concrete floor that looked like it had holes and cracks everywhere in it. Most of these "orphans" knew their parents. Their parents had given them up or sold them to somebody to pay their travel expenses to get to the orphanage. They came from places like Sudan and northeastern Nigeria and the parents knew it was better to send them away knowing they might never see them again then to have them stay there and possibly die. It was a very sad situation.

We gave them our donations, and they sang us some beautiful songs and danced for us. The "mother" of the orphanage pulled me up to dance with them in front of everyone. I didn't understand all the words to the songs but I heard God's name quite often and figured it was one of their traditional gospel songs. They wanted us to sing for them, so we sang "You are My Sunshine" and "I am a Child of God." They loved it!

Kaycee

The Living Hope Orphanage kids were mostly boys, but there were some girls. They were about twelve to sixteen years old. The director of the orphanage introduced us to them and they sang us a beautiful song and we all danced. You could just feel all the happiness and love in the room and it was amazing. I went into the girls' room and met eight beautiful girls. They showed me how they slept, on thin, two-inch mattresses just lying on the floor. It was hard to see.

When they braided my hair they all thought it was so pretty because it was blonde. We went back outside and handed out donations. When we had to leave, a fifteen year-old girl who had braided my hair followed us out to the bus. Her friends followed. They asked us when we were coming back and told them we would be back soon. Then they asked us "Tomorrow?" It was so cute. It was very hard to leave them.

Hanna

We had all brought bags of donated goods for them from the US. Things like toys, coloring books, clothes, soccer stuff, etc. It was so fun to see the kids' faces light up when we gave them our donations. They were all adorable. They sang a song and one boy recited lots of scripture verses he had memorized. It was a very cool experience. I hope I get to see those kids again some day

Alex

After the orphanage visit we went to another orphanage for children who were deaf or blind or mentally or physically challenged orphan children in Nigeria. If I had to describe this experience in one or two words, I would say, "HOPE." As soon as we pulled into the driveway of the orphanage we saw all of the young children dressed in red and white striped robes, crawling, playing in the dirt, eating the dirt, peeing, throwing up, hitting each other, biting each other, and no one doing anything about it. These kids were in the worst living conditions.

The so-called house was more or less an abandoned building and it was a wreck. The ceiling had holes in it; the floor was so dirty and the kids did not have the right equipment to be able to help them with their physical disabilities, such as a wheelchair. It was so hard to watch. I watched a little boy with both legs amputated crawling on his elbows through the dirt and up the stairs to get into the building. It broke my heart to see how little help he had and how much he was struggling, but no one could get him a simple wheelchair.

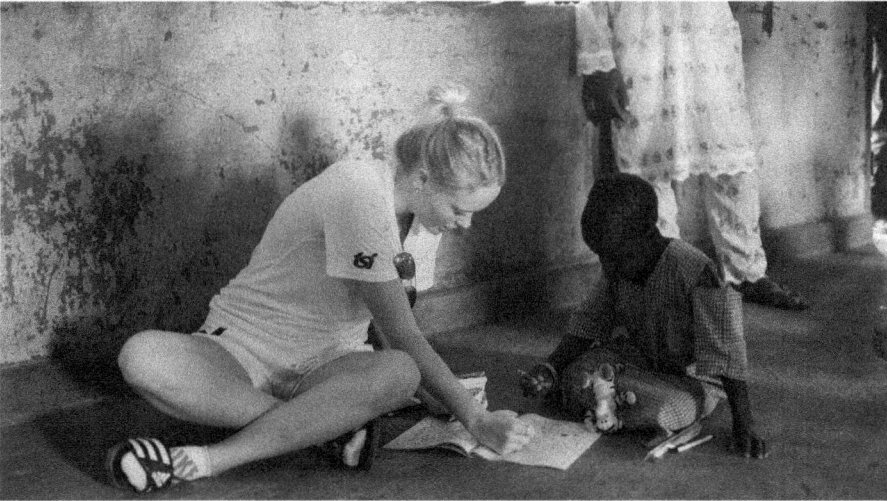

When we got inside the building, we tried to go talk to the kids and find ways to have fun with them. I saw a little boy with Downs Syndrome; he was one child who stuck out to me the most. I had him come over into the corner with me, and we colored together for more than twenty minutes. All I wanted for this kid, was for him to see that he was loved, even by one American girl who had never met him before. I wanted him to see that someone cared; someone cared enough to do something as simple as color a picture and crack jokes with him. This little boy stole my heart, and from that time on he was always right by my side. I made a special connection with this young boy. In the moment, getting down on the cement ground that was so dirty, a floor that I am sure had been pooped, peed, and thrown up on, wasn't a big deal. At that moment, I was present for him.

It was easy to sit there and color for twenty minutes; it was fun;

and it changed my life. The whole time he would tap my hand and point to the picture and just smile and laugh. I know that I changed his life and that I proved to him that people cared.

We all gathered in the main building and walked outside across a grassy area to go to the housing areas of the orphanage. The building was without a door, and when we walked in there were rows of bunk beds without sheets or pillows, just a plain plastic lined mattress and a bunk bed. The little boy was so excited to show me his bed; he kept pointing and grabbing me and saying, "This is mine, this is mine." They were so happy, and with so so little. It was amazing to see.

Britnee

The visit to the orphanage for children with physical disabilities was a horrible scene. There was a disabled boy who didn't have a wheelchair and was dragging his legs across the dirt and nobody was helping him. It troubled me that the government doesn't do more to help with the problems here. They showed us the children's rooms with bunk-bed cots. The kids were all so excited

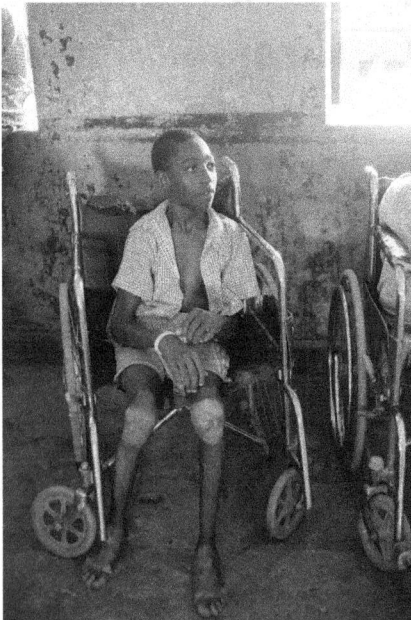

to show me their bed. When we handed out the donations they all fought over the coloring books. We heard news that after we left, some of the donations were taken away from the kids and sold. It makes me so sad that some people can be so cold-hearted.

Kaycee

At the orphanage we visited in the afternoon, I took a stuffed animal over to a child sitting in his wheelchair in the corner. When I handed it to him, I saw the most beautiful, heartwarming smile I had ever seen. He hugged it so tight and it almost made me cry how such a small thing could make him so happy.

I found another little boy and gave him a coloring book and some crayons. I sat down with him and showed him how each one looked different on the paper. We sat and colored together for almost twenty minutes. Then, he took me to show me his room. It was a low, long, hot building full of bunkbeds. I sat on his bed with him and we colored some more.

A different boy came over and was watching the boy color in the coloring book I had given to him. Then he took a crayon and wrote his name, the alphabet, and the numbers 1-10 and then he had the other boy copy him. It was amazing how patient he was even though he couldn't say a word. When the boy made a mistake, I asked him if he wanted a coloring book too, and he nodded his head. When I took it out of my backpack, tons of kids were grabbing at my backpack saying they wanted stuff, too. I gave out everything I had, but it wasn't enough. It was so sad because some kids didn't get anything, and they just looked so hurt.

Megan

At the second orphanage, I had to try very hard not to break down and cry after seeing the living conditions there. They were awful. There was one toilet and it was only a hole cut into the ground surrounded by scraps they salvaged for a wall. There were chickens running around the room. There was so much sickness in there it wasn't good for any of the kids.

It was completely unsanitary and unhealthy for them. Disease seemed to come with every breath and it broke my heart. The tour was an incredibly humbling and life-touching experience.

Bizzy

The tours of the orphanages were life-changing experiences. The kids there were so loving. It was just really amazing. We got to see how they lived and how little they had. I was so thankful for all the things I have now when I saw that their bathroom was a bucket, and they slept on the dirt floor every night with about twenty other people in a room smaller than my bedroom. They barely even fit in the room.

We went to an orphanage for disabled kids and that place was heartbreaking. The clothes they were wearing were ripped, torn and practically falling off of them. They had no air conditioning even when it was so hot outside. It was very sad.

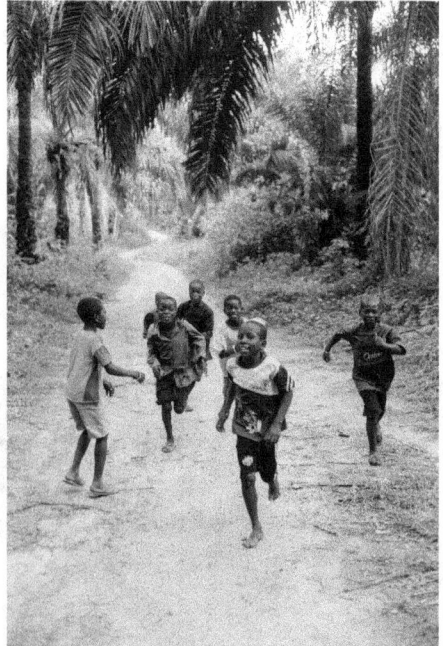

Hanna

At the home for the disabled kids I almost cried. It was so sad to see all those kids there. One boy kept hitting his head against the wall and biting himself. The kids were so cute and smiled when I handed them stuffed animals we had brought. I know this experience changed me in a lot of ways. It was so sad to see them, but I was also happy that we got to help these kids.

Hailey

The conditions at the second orphanage were one of the hardest things to see. I have never seen people treated so badly in my life. They had throw up all over them. Their kitchen was wide open with just one pot and a pile of dirty dishes with flies everywhere. It was a run-down building and it was really sad. We went to where they slept and there were chickens all over their beds just walking around.

Talk about unsanitary! But when we left I know it all left a huge mark on their hearts and ours. And just knowing life for them is always that way breaks my heart and humbles me.

VILLAGE

Alex

After the orphanage we went to a village in Ilesha. It was amazing, absolutely incredible. I loved every second of it. I didn't expect it to be what it was; it truly was a village of clay huts, in the middle of the forest. We drove deeper and deeper into the forest away from the main roads for quite a long time before we finally reached the end of the road and got to the village.

There was no such thing as driving down the street to the grocery store to get some food for the week. There was no such thing as going to the sink in the house and getting some water; instead they walked miles to find food and water. We toured their village and witnessed how they lived. There was no civilization besides their little village where they learned to survive. They lived off fruit and nuts growing on the trees, water from the pump, and who knows what else. The houses were all made out of clay. They were all very small, one-room homes that each had a worshipping spot. There was a chief of each village.

As we walked through the village, there was a time where we went through the forest, and the kids were running without any shoes over the rocks and sticks like it was no big deal, hitting each other with sticks, beating each other up and having so much fun in the process. It was so cool to see their way of playing with each other.

After awhile we sat on the benches in front of the chief's house, I decided to get some soccer balls out and play with the kids. I have never seen kids so happy to have one ball to chase around. It was amazing. They were so happy and content to fight over one ball even though there were so many kids. They never stopped chasing the ball and each other. One boy about my age to whom I had given a ball was hanging around as we were pumping up the balls. He asked me if I played soccer, and when I said yes, he was in shock because I was a girl. Right after, I sarcastically said, I would beat you one-on-one, and all of us just laughed and he said, "OK, Bring it on."

After passing out the balls and playing with the kids for a while, I brought a child a ball, and he asked, "Is this really for me? All mine?" He was so happy and so shocked that he was holding a ball that was really all for him.

Then we started playing one-on-one; it was so cool just to be able to mess around with the young boy and play soccer with him. He called it "American Girl against Black Boy." I absolutely loved being able to play with him, to be able to unite and join in something that meant so much to both of us.

After we handed out all of our other stuff to the kids, it was time for us get back onto the bus. Dickson was starting to get worried because when they saw all the stuff that we are giving away, they swarmed all around us. It was interesting to see how kind they were, but yet how much they pestered us about giving them things.

Britnee

The village was such a long way off the main road that I wondered how people even knew it existed. Very few people in the village spoke English, just the tribe leaders and storeowner. I quickly learned we could not communicate with them because they could not understand us. They were all amazed to see us and just stared. The moms threw their crying babies at us and just laughed at our surprised faces. There were SO many kids and they all followed us around like sheep. We were taken on a tour of the village and held hands with the youngest children.

The huts were made out of what looked like homemade bricks, bamboo, and mud. They had cocoa trees and oyster shells in a pond. We brought out the bracelets, and everyone went crazy.

We also brought out a few soccer balls and told them to share with each other. The lady who owned the only store in the village really liked me and followed me around. I gave her a ball and she was so happy. She asked me if I would marry and have babies with the tribe leader's seven year-old son. When we left she would say, "I'm going to miss you so much my friend!"

Kaycee

The visit to the village taught me how blessed we are but we're so unaware of it.

Megan

The kids were ADORABLE. We talked to everyone and tried to get to know them all and even though most of them didn't speak English, but it didn't matter to us. They were so excited to get anything we had for them. After that experience I realized that I take my life for granted and I know that I will never again be the same after this. My heart was forever touched by the wonderful people I met that day. I wanted to stay there forever.

Bizzy

The village was so cool. On the tour of the village and while we were on the tour I held hands with four beautiful children. Then we all played soccer with the little kids and gave them gifts. It was such a fun day.

Hailey

The drive to the village was beautiful and the trees everywhere reminded me of something out of *The Jungle Book* that I had read as a child. I loved it and the people there were so friendly! We held all the little babies. Most of the kids really liked to hold your hand when they gave us the tour. I will always remember seeing one old man's eye, it was really infected and oozing pus. It was blood shot and he looked like he was going blind. I really felt bad because he could tell I was looking at it, but it's something that will be really hard to forget!

Hanna

There were so many cute little kids running around the village! First they welcomed us. Everything was very pretty. We all grabbed a few of the kids' hands and they were "our" kids. They would not let go of our hands! It was so cute. The kids were really good at soccer. It was so fun and it was really hard to leave, but before we knew it, we had to. We left the village. It took about an hour to get back to the resort we were staying at.

GAME ON

Monday, March 31

Adam

The day of the game was here and I don't know about the girls but for me we had already accomplished so much that even though the game was the centerpiece of the mission, it sort of felt like an afterthought and less significant than all of the great work we had done in the previous two days. However, it was a blast. My team and the community there made this feel like the biggest match the girls had ever played in. It was like the Olympics or the World Cup and I had goose bumps as the girls all lined up before the match, put their hands over their hearts, and sang along to the instrumental version of our national anthem. As far as the score went, the game was a rout but the girls showed tremendous grit as they dealt with the oppressive heat, the huge crowd of at least four hundred locals, and the stage itself, which was unlike any these girls had ever played on let alone seen. I was also happy to see the relationships forged so quickly with their "opponents" in a true exchange of culture and nationality through such a simple sport as soccer.

Alex

The next morning, we had the game against some of the African girls in Nigeria—they were called the Osun Babes. And they were good. I remember pulling up to the field in the middle of Osun and thinking this couldn't be real. It was so green and such a pretty field, all gated with stadium bleachers. It was amazing.

The only problem was that as soon as we did one slow jog half-way down the field, we were all sweating like crazy. In case no one has mentioned it, Africa is so hot! As the game got closer, we were all pulled into the room underneath the stadium—my team and the other team. We lined up across from each other and just kind of stared at each other. It was cool just to be able to smile at them and see all the similarities that we had with one another and how much we all loved the game. They were all so intimidating at first, but we later learned that they were some of the sweetest girls. When it was time for the game to start, both of the teams and the referees walked onto the field and lined up. They announced our names and they played both national anthems. It was so cool to be able to be a part of that—to watch them as they sang their national anthem, to see the whole stadium stand with pride in their country and to stand there with my hand over my heart representing the United States.

It was an amazing experience. The stadium was packed with students and other members of the community. The game itself

was so fun! I loved every second of it even though we got completely destroyed and lost five to one. It was so awesome to be able to talk and laugh with all of the girls on the field. It wasn't a crazy, mean, or aggressive game.

The whole time we were giving compliments, and talking to each other about life, and laughing at mistakes, and making jokes. It was so cool to be able to join in a common love of soccer and interest with the girls.

Britnee

Today was our soccer game! Our team played really badly; the Nigerian girls dominated us on the field. They all had such good foot skills and had a very different style than our style of play. It was so hot I felt like I was dying. But to us, the score didn't really matter. We knew they were better than us, and we were just there to make friends and have fun. It was amazing to look around and think that we were in Africa playing a soccer game against Nigerians. There was an announcer who would make comments throughout the game like, "What a weak shot! Little effort from number 22!" It was pretty funny. They also played the same two songs over and over during the game.

When the game was over we talked to the girls. Some of them were twelve and others were nineteen. They said they felt blessed to have the opportunity to be on the team called the Osun Babes, because not many girls get the opportunity to play on a real team— or at all. Our favorite was a twelve-year-old girl named Abibat. She was absolutely adorable and wants to come to America someday. I hope she does. Some government officials gave us medals after the game, and everyone thanked us over and over for being there.

It took us a long time to leave the field because everyone wanted pictures with the American girls.

Kaycee

At the soccer game it was really fun to be with all of the girls from the other team. It was funny because the announcer for the game would say whatever popped into his head, so a lot of what he said sounded like criticism. There were a ton of people there watching the game. After the game, it was fun to go and talk to the girls.

A little boy who had broken his shoe in my dad's drill at the soccer clinic two days earlier came over and we gave him my cleats so he could play soccer. He never told me his name. I gave them to him and he said thanks and left. I did meet a boy named Alex. He had done my drill in the soccer clinic and needed shin guards. I asked my dad if I could give them away and he said sure. So I gave Alex my shinguards and he said thank you and ran off with his friends, then he turned around and said good-bye.

Maizy

Meeting and talking with the girls on the Osun Babes soccer team was an awesome experience. In Nigeria, sports are not popular among girls and are meant to be played by boys and men. Seeing these amazing soccer-playing girls who've trained incredibly hard proving that soccer is also a girl's sport was mind-changing. In America, we take equality as a right. Girls play sports. Girls get married when they want to. Girls start businesses. Girls receive education. However, in Africa, girls don't have the same rights or opportunities as we do and have a more controlled and pre-determined future. These girls, these young women soccer players, have proven that they can choose their own future, through soccer. I think that's the coolest thing ever.

Bizzy

The soccer game was so fun. Being able to play against a Nigerian team was such a wonderful opportunity. They were so good. Those girls were just determined and you could tell they really loved soccer.

Hanna

When we played the soccer game against the junior state team of Osun State, we lost by a lot. I was really frustrated at myself and at my team, but the team we played was amazing!

Hailey

Today we woke up and got ready to play the game of our lives! When we got to the field, I was shocked to see that we were going to be playing on grass! It was a very nice facility. We lined up before the match with the referee to check in. The other team was so serious. There wasn't a smile on any of the girls' faces. That's when I realized that this game wasn't just going to be a friendly. It seemed like life or death. We stepped out on the field, and shook hands. I started, and within the first five minutes I assisted a goal. It was called back for being offsides, but I was still pretty happy. I played well, but we got killed by the other team. They really do have natural talent. At the end of the game, it was like the whole team came alive, and they were so nice!!!

RELAXING AT ZENABAS

Alex

After the game we all went back to Zenababs just to sit and relax for the day. It was so fun just to hang around with some of the African workers; they were all so nice and they loved to listen to our music. We found that Justin Bieber is still a big deal over there. We went paddle boating, got a tour of the resort, and swam in the pool.

Britnee

We went to the pool at Zenababs' after our game to cool off. They played music for us and got out their brand new pool chairs just for us. We were a big deal down there. They played three songs by Justin Bieber and Celine Dion over and over that I guess they thought we would know. It was pretty funny.

After swimming the resort manager, Sesan, let us go catch catfish by hand. It was a lot of fun. He was so nice.

Hanna

At the resort, there was a catfish farm. There was a big tub just full of catfish and we would reach in and pick them up! It was hard cause they were all slippery. So some of the people got in the tub, (with the catfish) and handed them to us. Once we grabbed them, we would slide them around the tank! It was so funny. There was also a donkey and an ostrich farm. We ate the ostrich. It tasted and smelled like meatloaf.

GOING AWAY PARTY

Adam

This adventure was not just about soccer. It was about building relationships and inspiring each other. After the thrashing our girls took on the soccer field earlier in the day it was fantastic to see them put on their party shirts and have a uniquely fun time with their "opponents." The Nigerians definitely know how to party and I guarantee not one of the girls will soon forget the going away party they threw for us!

Alex

Later that night we all went to the party that our new friends threw for us. We all got to wear custom-made African shirts with the Save-A-Thon logo given to us by Adam's partner, Dickson. We just danced and ate some food. The food is hard to describe but fish, potatoes, and some kind of meat was provided. All of the girls from the soccer game were there along with a few others. It was so incredible to be able to dance together and have fun just like regular friends would do. It was cool to be able to look around and see all of us mesh together laughing and dancing.

They had an African dance group there that was great to watch, a comedian who was hilarious, and lots of interesting food. I remember I had to go to the bathroom really badly so we had to have bodyguards take us down the road a ways before we got to a bathroom. I remember there being no toilet paper, and we had to use leaves. It was crazy to me that something as simple as a bathroom wasn't near a big building. Towards the end of the party, we all were able to get African names from the woman who was the master of ceremonies. It was interesting to see what names they gave to each of us. When it was my turn, she gave me the name of Bolonle, which means "wealth in your life." After the party was over we headed back home to Zenabas and started packing. The next morning we headed to the airport for our flight to Houston.

Britnee

We arrived an hour and a half late to our going away party but were still the first ones there. Apparently, Nigerians are not as concerned with time as we are in America. We danced to some African music with the hostess and some of the African girls. They fed us some strange foods, like turkey gizzards as an appetizer and peppe rice (which I found out after I ate it that this means really, really spicy rice) and a whole fish with scales and fins still on it for dinner. The African girls were taking huge bites of the scaly fish, while some African traditional drummers and dancers entertained us.

Then we all received our African names one by one on stage. My name was Obocosalaw. It means "Honeydrop"- sweet, rich, and spreads her sweetness wherever she goes. All the kids kept asking if they could have our shirts (we were wearing traditional African keshas) and our cleats. It was hard to say no.

Kaycee

The Nigerian name they gave to me, Laka, means strong and powerful.

Hailey

I'm worn out and ready to go home. At the send-off party we danced, and they served us really unusual food and gave us a fish that was practically raw. My Nigerian name was Aduche, which means beauty and showing beauty in others. It was a fun little party and a nice goodbye!

Hanna

At the party with the team we played earlier we all went up onto the stage and danced. My African name was Arewa: beautiful. The party was a fun and really good experience.

LAST DAY

Tuesday, April 1

Adam

Like all of the best trips and adventures in my life they always seem to end far too quickly. We had gotten back to our rooms very late the night before after a full day of the soccer match, swimming, and party. So, I remember waking up Tuesday morning was a bit rough, at least for me. The day ahead would include packing, sneaking in a visit to another orphanage, feeding some monkeys and making the long, crazy ride to the airport.

Despite the fact that some of the girls, and some of the adults, were a little beat up from the previous day (sunburns, sore muscles, a twisted ankle) they were all champs. In fact, I sometimes had to catch up with the adults as their energy and enthusiasm for the mission was so great they kept things moving nonstop with new ideas and requests to do things. I am grateful for the bonds we created and for their great help without which this trip wouldn't have made nearly the same impact it did on all of us.

Britnee

Today we start our journey home. This trip went by way too fast, and I wish I could stay longer. Their culture was so much different than ours and adjusting to it was the hardest part. In the morning we packed, said goodbye to Zenababs and Sesan and then headed over to a baby orphanage.

This was a heartbreaking experience for me. To see these babies anywhere from ten days old to three years who had been abandoned by their parents made me so sad. How could anyone leave these precious things, their own babies? They all just wanted to be held and loved the whole time. Emmanuel, the baby I first held, was being adopted that day. They said he was three weeks old, and he was such a tiny baby. It made me so happy to know that he was getting a home and a family. It's hard to think about these kids living in orphanages that might stay there until they are 18 because they don't ever get adopted and then don't have a family. It broke my heart. It was really hard to leave them, and I wanted to take them all home with me. Visiting the orphanage made me want to adopt someday.

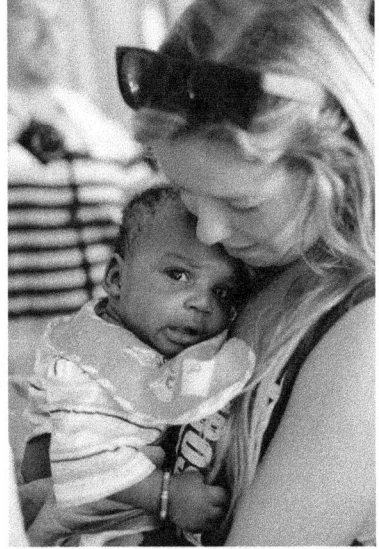

Kaycee

Today was our last day. In the morning we woke up and went to a baby orphanage. As soon as we arrived, I fell in love with a two-month-old baby girl, Fallenzentina. She was a beautiful girl and her smile was adorable. She actually kept looking up at me and smiling.

I wanted to take her home, but I couldn't. It was sad how young all of the kids were, and they didn't have parents. Also, two of them had Cerebral Palsy. It was so sad because they just had to lie there and couldn't do anything.

The kids had bad circumstances. The building was small and very hot. But they all had cribs so that was good. It was very hard for me to leave all the kids.

Bizzy

The baby orphanage was such a cool experience. They had such beautiful babies there. They were so cute. I cried when I had to put my baby down and leave because she gave me the biggest smile and that just made me cry more. I really wanted to take that little girl home and take her out of that hot orphanage and take her to a nice house with nice clean clothes and help get her an education. But knowing I couldn't was really hard for me.

There were so many babies and only two women taking care of them. I really hope those babies have a good life.

After the orphanage, and with very little time in our schedule, we stopped by the Osun-Osogbo Sacred Grove. Unfortunately, we didn't have time to visit the park but at the entrance there were hundreds of white-throated monkeys running around and we stopped to feed them.

It was so cool! There were so many little monkeys just running around wild, and we got to feed them bananas right out of our hands.

As we were leaving the people that run the park tried to charge us $300 for our ten minute stay because they knew we were Americans and wanted to take advantage of us. Adam paid them much less than what they were asking so the "shake-down" would stop and we could head to the airport to make our flight.

Hailey

Today we are leaving Nigeria. It's time to go home! The airport took FOREVER and it felt a little like a death march. My ankle was gigantic because I found out I had sprained it. It wasn't too bad but being on it all day long and standing at the airport made it swell and it turned black and blue. When I hurt it in the game Mitch (my coach) told me to suck it up. I probably should have come out but chose to suck it up. I am glad I did because I am so thankful I got to play all game and have the time of my life!

When we arrived home (after 24 hours of traveling), the first thing I did was hop into the shower. It was definitely the best shower I have ever had in my life. But more than being grateful for a hot shower I am so glad I shared these experiences with others in my life. It was humbling, heart warming, eye-opening, and absolutely amazing!

Britnee

Leaving the airport in Lagos took so long. We stood in the immigration and security lines for well more than an hour and almost missed our flight. I was overjoyed to eat an American meal when we landed in Houston.

WRAPPING UP

Adam

When you do something like this trip and see so many things, meet so many new people, and experience so many feelings you want to bottle them up and keep the bottle nearby so you can take a sip of the experience again and again as "regular" life continues back home and you feel the memories of the trip fade a bit.

This book is the best way I can think of to keep the impact of the experience fresh and ensure the lessons learned change all involved for the long-term. Save-A-Thon For Africa is a long-term project that my family and I will likely do until we die or simply can"t do it anymore. There is so much work to do and the good that comes from this work is the stuff of life that matters and brings the greatest rewards and satisfaction.

In order to maximize the benefit to these young American women and everyone who has the privilege to know them I asked them some questions to really make them think about this experience and how they can use it throughout their lives for good. I have selected their most poignant thoughts and insights and include them here on the final pages of this book. I am grateful for their efforts and goodness. I think you will be, too.

OBSERVATIONS

Kaycee

When I got home from Nigeria it was crazy how just seeing how the smallest thing could make me so happy. The trip has shown me that we Americans have such an easy life, but we take it for granted and always think it should be better. Most people aren't happy with what they have, but they have so much more than other people. And I've seen that first hand now. The people in Nigeria had so little but were so happy.

We can learn so much from them. And I hope by going on this trip, I didn't only learn how I should act in my daily life and how I should be grateful for everything, but I want to know that I made a difference in the lives of all the children we met.

Kylie

My favorite thing about Africa is the people. Everyone is so friendly and wants to be around you, which is the best feeling. I love the people we met and their culture, the food they eat, the way they drive, speak, and make money for their families.

Life here is just so interesting to me. It's crazy to think about how different Africa is from the US and other developed countries.

When I was in Africa, I saw things that make me so sad such as seeing little kids' bellies bloated with hunger, malnourishment, and motherless or abandoned babies. Despite all of these hardships that these people have to endure, I have never seen happier people and that has sparked an inspiration inside myself that makes me so grateful for everything I have.

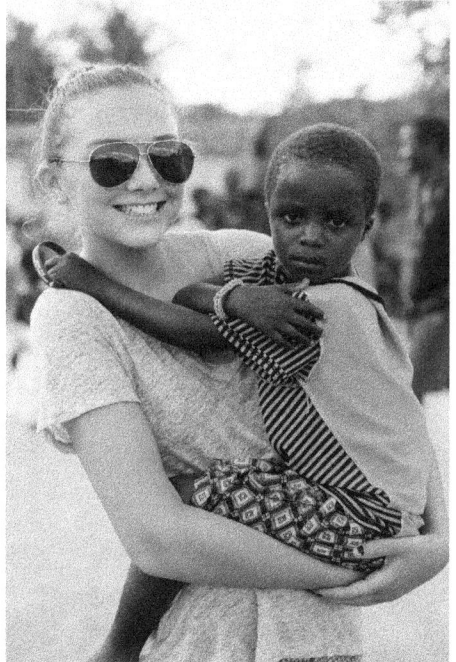

Kids will tell me that they want to come to America all the time. At a soccer clinic we held to launch the project in February 2014, with my dad, Lindsi Lisonbee Cutshall, Nano Norris, and our photographer Travis Richardson, a little boy told me that he wanted to play soccer in America but said he has no opportunity to do so.

Although that broke my heart to hear an eight year old say this, it made me that much more grateful to have this opportunity to play soccer in Nigeria. It also has inspired me to do my best to inspire other young African kids to work hard to be able to accomplish their goals; whether it has to do with soccer or not.

It's always good to be home, but Africa is one of my favorite places in the world and I always want to stay longer. Something I would be interested in doing later in my life would be living in Africa for a few months. That would be such an amazing thing to be able to experience more of how the locals live over there, and I love being around the people so it would be so awesome to be able to hangout with them more.

We changed so many lives over there in so many ways, but I think the best thing we accomplished on this journey was making these beautiful kids feel loved and making them know that someone 8,000 miles away loved and cared for them more than we could every explain. I think that's a feeling everyone deserves. It's about hope.

Noheli

I loved the people so much! They were so humble and nice to us. They would call us beautiful and touch our hair. I felt wonderful and I loved being around them.

When we were in the bus we would wave at them and they would wave back with big beautiful smiles on their faces. I didn't want to go home but I was eager to see my family.

I loved the people. I felt like a celebrity there and I wished it would never end. I loved helping the people.

I did a lot of service but honestly I learned more from them than they did from me. I have everything here and they have learned how to live with so little. They are more humble, kind and grateful for what they have.

It made me more grateful for the things I have and the little things I thought were not that important. It made me grateful for water that I have whenever I want or need it.

Britnee

I think the first step in making Africa a better place is to make a better government. The government isn't helping the orphanages to the best of their ability, or even at all. The deaf, blind, and disabled orphanage is in desperate need of wheelchairs and sanitary supplies. When we visited the secretary to the governor's office, he had stacks of wheelchairs not being used. If the government started to help the people more, that would make a huge change. The mindset of the country also needs to change and that will take a lot of effort.

But one thing that we as Americans can do to help Nigeria is to change our perspective of them and their country. It's not all bad! I think there is a lot of good there and we need to see them as a country that's trying its best to get on its feet and progress in the world. We can help them by continued humanitarian efforts and giving our support to those who are trying to make it a better place, like Adam's Bridges to America.

If there's one thing this trip has taught me, it's how proud I really am to be an American. America is amazing. We don't have a corrupt government; we have rules and laws to keep us safe. We have freedom and don't have to fear being invaded. We are very lucky to have what we have and I'm so grateful to be born in the US.

I'm relieved to be back in America but I already miss Africa! I miss the experiences and the people I met there and the beautiful weather.

I would love to go back, especially since I know a lot more about the culture and how to adjust. I hope I did a lot of good in Africa and helped to better some lives. I really hope I helped those teenage girls realize that they don't have to let the boys push them around like they do. They are just as amazing as the boys. I'm excited to see what happens with the Bridges Cup with the teams they are bringing over to America. A chance to come to America would be an amazing experience for them.

This Africa trip truly changed my life. It made me realize how blessed I am, how much I have to be grateful for, and how proud I am to be an American. To live in a place where people dream of going to and we take it for granted. It made me realize that not everyone in the world thinks and acts the way we do. I learned about a whole new culture. I never thought I would get such an amazing experience and I'm so happy I did. I can't wait to see how else I can help change people's lives!

Alex

I can honestly say that the people in Africa changed my life. It was the most incredible experience. If I could go back today, tomorrow, yesterday or any other day in the year, I would pack my bags and go with no questions about it.

People kept telling me that it was a risk and that it was dangerous, and it may just have been because of our security measures 24/7 that I never felt threatened. I never was scared. I was so amazed, and happy to be there.

I would be standing off to the side,

watching people interact and I would just start crying. Africa truly is the most incredible place, with so many incredible people and values. Yes, they don't have a lot of money; they don't have a perfect govern- ment to rule them; they don't have all of these things that make them a perfect country; but it is because they are different. And different is ok, different is good, and different is what makes it AFRICA.

Tabitha

As the end of our journey grew nearer and nearer, the days sped by faster and faster. I missed my family and friends so much but I would have done anything to stay just at least one day longer. I felt like I left part of my heart there with those amazing people and as leaving day drew closer my heart broke a little more each day.

This trip has been so inspiring and life changing that words can't even describe how I feel, no matter how hard I try. I know I didn't make Africa perfect or fix all or really any of its problems but my dream for them is that more people like the group of amazing girls I went with will get interested and will want to help make a difference. If we can keep it going, one day we will break through and we can help make it a better place for the people who live there.

Being home is definitely bitter sweet. I had to leave so many great friends to go to Africa but I had to leave so many to come back home as well. It's hard to transition back to everyday life. It was really different going to school and not having everyone crowd around me. But it was nice to smell how clean everyone was and to get to see my friends and family again, waiting for me with open arms. There is no way that I'm not going back. There are so many more things that I feel like I could do if I just had more time. If I could I would go there every week, without a doubt. I love it there and I miss it already.

Going on this trip has been a real eye-opener and has helped me see how lucky I am to live in this beautiful country. I have learned not to take for granted the little things because a lot of people don't even have what we have. My experience has taught me to see what is really important in life and to realize that I have so much. I may have not saved someone's life or made a drastic difference to their lives like they did to mine but if nothing else, I wanted everyone I met to know that somewhere out there, even if they are 8,000 miles away, that I care for them, each and every one of them. I love them all.

Going on this trip showed me that with hard work and dedication anything can happen. It has helped to show me that I can do hard things if I stick with it and have hope. I know that no mountain is high enough to back down from. You can make it to the top and you can do amazing things. It has showed me that trying new things is worth it and if you know it is the right thing to do, you can do it.

Hanna

I remember everything so clearly from the trip including what the food we ate smelled like, what we did, who we met, and how nice everyone was. I hope I never forget the details of our amazing trip.

I want to go back so badly! Like really, right now. Lying in my bed, I'm remembering all the little details, and everything on this trip was so perfect. I wish I could've done more.

The experience was amazing! I'm sure everyone who went would say the same thing! I loved every second of it and honestly, if I could, would live there forever! I can't wait to go back!

Maizy

On our trip to Nigeria I didn't cure malaria or anything, but I think I helped start something amazing, and it definitely left a huge impact on me. I'm hoping this impact was also left on others as well.

This experience has changed my life is so many ways. It really helped open my eyes as to what's going on out there in this big bad world that we live in. Also it showed me that there is good in the bad, and that we're all just people surviving in the good and bad.

Some of us are less fortunate than others. Some of us have way more than we could ever wish for. That's just how life works. In Africa, there are these little kids that have fun with sticks everyday. Or soccer. Guess what?

They love it. They love playing soccer everyday. They look forward to that. Those kids don't care if they don't have new Nike cleats, or if their hair looks good. They just want to go out and play. That's what really changed my life.

Megan

I left my heart in Nigeria for sure. The people are great and I miss being there. It was an amazing experience and I hope I can go back as soon as possible.

I LOVE AFRICA!

DICKSON AS TOLD TO ADAM

I am extremely proud to be part of Sav-A-Thon for Africa. I love working with Adam Miles on this noble project for the people of my country. We have had a lot of ups and downs getting this project off the ground, but the results have been so positive. Save-A-Thon for Africa is all I want to do!

When these American girls played their historical match against Osun Babes in Nigeria in April 2014 the announcer played the song: "Stand Up for the Champions." Well, I stand up for these girls who, despite their steep loss to the Nigerians that day, are the real champions.

I remember sitting with them in the hot locker room at half-time. The girls were exhausted and down four to zero (4-0) or something like that. Even though these are talented, competitive young women the score didn't matter to them. They played hard in the match, and on foreign soil they were fighting oppressive heat, jet lag, and the natural pressure of representing their home country. To me, they were gladiators!

Even now, when I think of how far they came for this very moment, to serve the youth of Nigeria, I am deeply touched. When I consider how much they sacrificed to be there away from family and the comforts and safety of America, almost entirely paid for with funds they each raised, I truly am grateful to be associated with this project and these amazing young women.

I have no doubt that great things are in store for these young women and the many lives they will touch in their rich futures ahead.

ONE LAST THOUGHT ON DICKSON

At the end of our journey, which went by way too fast, I was sitting near Dickson in the front of the our bus full of exhausted, but excited young ladies as we approached the Lagos Airport. My girls, Kylie and Marissa, tapped my elbow and said, "Dad, what's wrong with Dickson?"

I looked at Dickson's face and saw tears running down his cheeks. I was pretty sure I knew the cause of those tears, but I asked him anyway: "Dickson, what's wrong?"

His answer was classic Dickson: noble, humble and sensitive. "I am so proud of these girls and am going to miss them all very much."

That caused more than a few tears in our section of the bus. What a fitting and meaningful end for my girls and me to know that the life of this amazing man had also been deeply touched by this experience! My girls to this day talk about him daily and how much they love and admire him.

As we all reluctantly left Nigeria, with mostly empty suitcases, having given away our gifts and belongings, our hearts were overflowing with love and respect for and an understanding of the good people and culture of Nigeria.

Dickson would stay behind for weeks.

Dickson had put his full-time job back in the United States on hold and risked being able to provide for his family, but he was so determined to continue the journey and make the Save-A-Thon vision a reality.

Somehow, I went back to Osun State in May 2014 to launch the Bridges Cup to nearly one hundred school administrators and coaches. This took place in the wake of the Chibok Girls kidnapping by Boko Haram which sparked the global hashtag: #BringBackOurGirls.

While I was there for a few days I realized just how fortunate we were to have sneaked in our trip with these American girls before all of this attention and concern broke out for Nigeria. I am convinced that had this tragedy happened before our visit some or most of the girls, would have canceled their trip due to fears about safety.

After I left, Dickson insisted on staying to work on getting the funds from the government as partners for our project. Despite both of us meeting the Governor and receiving his assurances that we would, indeed, receive the funding, the only thing I received was news that Dickson had gotten malaria. He was treated quickly and effectively, but in his weakened state, nearly homeless, and not eating well due to the severe money shortage, he caught some sort of infection. I had had enough. I gave him an ultimatum that he had to use the return ticket in the next few days which had already been extended a couple of times and get home or he would have to find a way home by himself. That seemed to do it, and he finally relented after giving nearly everything he had, including his own life. A couple of days after getting home to California, I got a call from his sweet, supportive wife that he was in the ER for several days with pneumonia. He was so sick that I couldn't talk to him for a few days, and my heart ached to think of the pain that this amazing friend, partner, and brother was enduring from fighting so hard and so selflessly for our cause.

Thankfully, after outstanding treatment from the doctors in California he recovered and bounced back. If he had stayed in Nigeria, he would have surely died from pneumonia and he was grateful that I persisted in getting him home to his family in California.

What a dedicated man! What a testament to perseverance and resilience he is and a model for our girls who made the trip with him. Save-A-Thon for Africa and We Are One would not be here today without Dickson Egbukonye!

For that, we are truly grateful to him!

CONCLUSION

This trip was really the tipping point for Save-A-Thon for Africa. It was the catalyst that caused Dickson to essentially risk his life and stay behind and caused me to go back and make a big promise to hundreds of Nigerian youth. The promise was that we would hold the Bridges Cup in Osun State, Nigeria this year.

Dickson and I had every intention of keeping that promise and

worked very hard to do just that. Unfortunately, things beyond our control started to emerge and made keeping that promise look exceedingly difficult.

I focused on the reasons why we couldn't make the Cup happen this year. Here was my list:

-State government funding never materialized;

-Boko Haram kidnapping of the Chibok Girls;

-Osun State Gubernatorial election chaos;

-Ebola outbreak in West Africa;

-Work demands for both Dickson and me.

I found myself giving in to this list and rationalizing that the hundreds of kids would surely understand if we didn't hold the Cup. They would survive, as they always seemed to…most of them anyway when others broke their promises.

Then it hit me.

116

When I formally announced the Bridges Cup in May 2014 to dozens of coaches, teachers, and players I wasn't just promising hundreds of kids that we would host the Cup. I was unconsciously raising the bar of integrity in Nigeria. I was getting the hopes up of thousands of African kids that we would actually keep our word. In a country, an entire continent for that matter, with so many empty or broken promises I realized that if I didn't keep my word and find a way to do this that I would be a part of this vicious cycle of big words and no action.

So, in September 2014, with the craziness of the Osun State gubernatorial election over, Nigeria being declared "Ebola free" by the World Health Organization, Dickson and I decided we had a tight window in which we could keep our promise and do this.

Dickson's wife was pregnant with their third child and first baby girl. The Nigerian Presidential elections were scheduled for early February 2015 that I was sure would prove to be even more chaotic and unsettling than the State elections were. So, within this tight window I declared the list of excuses above dead and we moved forward!

The Bridges Cup took place in Osun State Nigeria with more than 30 registered teams. My wife, Wendy, our photographer, Travis, and I joined Dickson for a weekend in November 2014 to watch the semi-final matches and conduct an award presentation.

We did it! We kept the promise. Over 30 teams (about 500 kids) now had the chance to participate in the inaugural Bridges Cup.

We took the matches through the semi-finals for the boys and the girls. The finals will be held in Nigeria next spring (2015) after the elections have been settled and the country has returned to normalcy and stability, insomuch as that exists in Nigeria.

The winning girls' and boys' teams will then make preparations to come to Utah for a week of mind-opening activities including friendly soccer matches with local teams, and visits to schools, businesses and cultural attractions in the state.

We will likely never receive the promised funding from the State but that's OK. Once I decided that chasing down the funds was a huge waste of time, effort, and emotional capital doors have been opened and Dickson and I have become free to make this event happen on our terms. (Many thanks to my long-time friend and wise advisor, David Sessions, for helping me see the light and giving me the courage to make a hard decision to move forward without the government.)

In addition to providing hundreds of African kids the chance to show their talents and have the chance of a lifetime to come to America, we are also showing millions of adults, including these kids' parents and leaders, that integrity matters. We wanted to prove that there are still people who practice and benefit from integrity and fulfill their promises even under difficult circumstances.

How can we expect, or even just hope, that the youth of Africa's most populous nation will learn integrity and choose a life of hard work, honesty, and trust if we were not willing to act and keep our promises? Who else will cure the country, and maybe even the continent, of corruption and dishonesty if not the African youth?! They need this.

The world needs this and we believe the youth there, with help and support from the youth in the USA can do this.

We ARE One!

As you've reached the end of this book I am really happy to tell you that these stories actually represent just the first chapter of a much longer book of work that I believe will fundamentally change the lives of thousands of people who embrace this opportunity. We will keep writing this longer "book" by continuing to make and keep promises.

You've read authentic, heart-felt accounts from a special group of courageous, compassionate, and driven young women. These stories haven't all been pretty or even surprising but these girls have shared with you their experiences that many thought they would never have. These are primarily white, middle class, Christian girls from Utah who crossed thousands of miles to a country that is often, usually justifiably, viewed as a rough (at best) and dangerous (at worst) place filled with unsavory and dishonest hustlers. But you've seen that there is much good in the youth there and many opportunities to do even better in Nigeria, Africa's most populated country and largest economy.

I would argue that the work these girls did in less than a week with hundreds of Nigerian kids was more effective than any government program out there in bridging race, status, religion, and gender. Lives were touched and minds and hearts opened to different ways of living life. The one thing that binds these youth is the desire to be better.

In the wake of some contentious times in the USA I reflect on race relations in our country and realize how much work there is to do here. But the great message of this story is that we are, indeed, one! The girls have learned that race, gender, and status don't matter when it comes to soccer. With enough hard work, persistence, and opportunity these kids can become great. And if they can become great at soccer, a sport virtually anyone can play, then they can take those lessons learned and apply them to education, business, humanitarian work, etc. and truly change the world. I don't care if these kids, African or American, become the next Hope Solo, Marta, Messi, or Ronaldo. I care that they become the best that *they* can become.

If you have been touched by anything in this book and want to help us further our cause then do any or all of the following:

1. Share your thoughts about the book on social media with your network. You can stay in touch with us by liking our Facebook page at http://www.facebook.com/weareonebook;

2. Buy this book for a friend, team or family member, a teacher, a coach. You can find it on Amazon.

3. Donate whatever you can to our effort and support life-changing opportunities to sponsor a player or even a team to continue to be involved in this mutual exchange of a love of soccer. Even better? Come with us to Nigeria! Visit http:// saveathonforafrica.org to learn more and donate.

We Are One is our story to tell the world about how a few girls had the chance to bring their love of soccer to Nigeria and make fast friends.

Now they want to invite other Nigerian girls and boys back to visit them in the USA and experience the deep and lasting benefits that come from being united despite being different colors and cultures. I believe we made a difference for the future of race relations through a mutual love of soccer.

You can be a part of this very unique venture.

As long as we are able we will continue to take groups to Nigeria to witness Save-A-Thon in action and get the chance to see the Bridges Cup personally, while performing service in schools, villages and orphanages.

It's not too soon to start preparations; fundraising, shots, passports visas, etc.

Get in touch with me about the chance to go see the effort for yourself at adam@bridgestoamerica.org

Thank you for taking the time to read We Are One and supporting Save-A-Thon For Africa.

Adam Miles, Founder

TIMELINE

2004

Bridges To America reunification services unofficially launches.

July 2010

Dickson Egbukonye family reunited from Nigeria to USA.

March 2012

Bridges To America founder, Adam Miles, and eldest daughter, Mikaelyn, visit Ghana, West Africa for first time, meet boy named Borges in remote village and promises to return with daughter Kylie and bring soccer balls for him and all his friends.

April 2012

Miles returns to USA and tells 12-year old, daughter, Kylie, about idea to use soccer to help and inspire African youth. She enthusiastically responds and Save-A-Thon For Africa is born.

December 2012

Miles returns to Ghana with Kylie and middle daughter, Marissa then 17, to keep Save-A-Thon promise. The trio visits hundreds of kids delivering food, treats, soccer balls and smiles. Save-A-Thon grows up.

Spring 2013

Dickson visits Adam and pitches idea of launching Save-A-Thon

For Africa in his homeland, Nigeria. Adam is initially skeptical but decides to take exploratory trip to Nigeria with Dickson, in the Fall.

October 2013

Adam takes first trip to Nigeria and falls in love with the people, and the craziness and risks of Africa's most populated country. The huge economic and humanitarian opportunities to execute his philosophy of doing so much with so little in Africa become a reality and keep him coming back to work with his new partner and brother, Dickson developing the most impactful way to launch Save-A-Thon For Africa in Nigeria.

February 2014

Joined by co-founder and daughter, Kylie Miles, pro US women soccer players, Lindsi Lisonbee Cutshall and Natalie "Nano" Norris, travel with Adam and professional photographer, Travis Richardson to Osun State Nigeria to officially launch Save-A-Thon For Africa.

March/April 2014

13 young American women soccer players and a handful of coaches and chaperones head to Nigeria to play and coach soccer as well as provide humanitarian service.

April 2014

Radical Islamist terrorist group, Boko Haram, brazenly kidnaps more than 200 schoolgirls in Northeastern Nigeria and the world starts to focus its attention on the growing conflict in Nigeria with the #BringBackOurGirls campaign.

As of Summer 2014 the girls have still not been found.

May 2014
The inaugural Bridges Cup is announced in Osun State providing
a unique opportunity for Nigerian youth to compete against each
other in soccer. The grand prize of a free weeklong trip to the
USA to play soccer against American youth and visit American
schools and businesses attracts hundreds of youth to the
tournament.

July 2014
First case of Ebola in Nigeria is discovered as West Africa deals
with the worst outbreak of the deadly disease in decades.

August 2014
State Governor elections in Osun State create unstable and unsafe
environment for local citizens and foreigners.

October 2014
Nigeria is declared Ebola-free and the dust from the elections has
mostly settled.

With no assistance from the State government that was long-
promised, Adam and Dickson decide to move forward with the
Bridges Cup anyway.

November 2014
Over 30 soccer teams comprised of talented young women and
men play hard but peacefully in the first ever, Bridges Cup in
Osun State. Two semi-finals teams (female and male) were
determined and will play in the Bridges Cup Finals in Spring 2015.

December 2014

We Are One, a book documenting the adventures of Save-A-Thon
For Africa as seen through the eyes of the American young women
who braved multiple challenges, stereotypes, and fears to play
their sport against their Nigerian sisters, is launched.

*Can't wait to see what our future timelines will look like with
your continued support!*

www.ingramcontent.com/pod-product-compliance
Lightning Source LLC
Chambersburg PA
CBHW050357280326
41933CB00010BA/1498